Are There Too Many Lawyers? and Other Vexatious Questions

Joseph S. Fulda

The Foundation for Economic Education
Irvington-on-Hudson, New York 10533

About the Author

Joseph S. Fulda holds five academic degrees in the life and mathematical sciences and has held faculty positions in schools of arts and science, engineering, continuing education, and medicine. He has written for *The Freeman* since 1981 and has published some 90 articles, notes, and reviews. Dr. Fulda's work for *The Freeman* has been reprinted as op-ed's in numerous newspapers and in three languages.

Published April 1993
ISBN 910614-84-9

To My Parents with Love

Foreword

Economists cannot tell us what we should do and how we ought to act. As theorists searching for inexorable principles of human action they abstain from making judgments of value and prescribing any goal or purpose in life. But they can tell us what we must do if we want to achieve our chosen objectives and what means we must employ to attain them. Economists can demonstrate, for instance, how we must act in order to find employment if that's our goal or how we can grow in income and wealth if that should be our aim. Economists may even reflect on the consequences of our actions depending on the means we choose to employ.

Goal and purpose are what give life meaning and their absence make it dreary and empty, which explains why economists generally are a tedious lot. Yet some economists briefly leave their theoretical platform by making one simple valuation and choosing one ultimate end: the preservation of human life and improvements in the conditions of life. He who favors economic growth and rising standards of living does not speak as an economic theorist but as a philosopher who reflects on human conditions. He returns to the economic stage when he deliberates on the means he may use for the attainment of his chosen ends.

Dr. Joseph S. Fulda is such a philosopher-economist. His thought-provoking essays and articles make it very clear that, to him, the aim of life is to live and serve, and to live means to be aware, joyously and serenely, of the many problems of life. This very foundation of the Fulda writings makes this collection so extraordinary and fascinating.

For students taking an introductory economics course,

this book may serve ideally as a supplement to the main text. For students examining current economic issues, the book offers an excellent introduction to the problems and issues of our time. For the general reader the book is ideal in generating interest in the study of economics. It provides a framework of basic analysis which is so useful in the study of all other economic and social phenomena. The reader must be warned, however, that the range of topics is not complete nor is the Fulda treatment of the topics exhaustive. He merely covers a few vital issues and analyzes their essence and significance. We are hopeful that he will want to expand both the range and the analysis for future editions of this stimulating collection.

—Hans F. Sennholz

Preface

To my mind, there is a cause. That cause is freedom.
—Senator Barry Goldwater[1]

The philosophy of freedom is a simple one: Force is not to be used as a means to an end, however noble and grand the end might seem. Only in self-defense may the sword be unsheathed or the gun unholstered. Force cannot bring about happiness, prosperity, or virtue—the three ideals in whose name force has most often been applied. Only free associations between people make for happiness; only free human action creates things of value; and, only the free choices of free citizens can be moral.

You may wonder at such childlike fascination with and love of freedom. "After all," you might say, "freedom is not magic." Surely not. But equally surely, the next best thing. People and the creativity they possess are the only magic we have, the only road to better lives, material and spiritual, always on America's horizon:

> I must study politics and war that my sons may have liberty to study mathematics and philosophy. My sons ought to study mathematics and philosophy, geography, natural history, naval architecture, navigation, commerce and agriculture, in order to give their children a right to study painting, poetry, music, architecture, statuary, tapestry and porcelain.[2]

Indeed, the love of freedom explains this book, for I am an amateur—in its original sense of one who undertakes a work out of love, rather than as a professional obligation. I hold five academic degrees, but all of these are in the mathematical and life sciences; I have served on faculties of arts and science, engineering, continuing education, and medicine, but each appointment has been in the mathematical and life sciences. The market will now tell me whether my writings on matters relating to freedom, writings which span more than a decade and on which I have labored for countless hours, make a valuable contribution to the literature of liberty.

We intend three such contributions. In the first unit, we provide a scholarly exposition of the first principles of the freedom philosophy. Our aim here is to be sophisticated yet simple, abstract yet accessible. In the second unit, we present a dozen case studies of freedom and statism in action. These case studies explore varied issues by the light of the principles illuminated in the first unit. Our aim here is to be lively yet serious, thorough yet concise. In the very brief third unit, we discuss the unsettling recent phenomenon of the misapplication and overapplication of ethical principles to everyday human living and how this conflicts with human freedom and dignity.

Nevertheless, the reader is reminded that this is an anthology, not a monograph. A monograph might promise to take a question or a set of related questions and surround it until by the book's close, everything the author wishes to say about the subject is exhausted. But an anthology is a set of previously written essays organized using an appropriate classification scheme (in this case: foundations, case studies, and the overapplication of ethics in public life). Such classifications are intended to cover all the essays in the unit, but the subject of the unit is not intended to be exhausted by its contents. Because, however, the editor of this anthology is also the author of the individual contributions, an effort has been made to significantly edit the pieces in such a way as to allow a smooth and coherent reading experience, and in that way, this work lies somewhere in between a true anthology and a monograph. Nevertheless, there is no representation that such large and lifelong areas of study and thought as we treat here are or can be exhausted by our twenty-six contributions. As philosopher Robert Nozick said in the preface of his acclaimed *Anarchy, State and Utopia*:

> One view about how to write a philosophy book holds that an author should think through all the details of the view he presents, and its problems, polishing and refining his view to present to the world a finished, complete, and elegant whole. This is not my view. At any rate, I believe that there is also a place and a function in our ongoing intellectual life for a less complete work, containing unfinished presentations, conjectures, open questions and problems, leads, side connections, as well as a main line of argument. There is room for words on subjects other than last words.[3]

This work, surely, is long enough to be open to criticism that it is not long enough! *Tant mieux*.

—JOSEPH S. FULDA
NEW YORK, NEW YORK

---

1. Barry Goldwater, *With No Apologies* (Morrow, 1979), p. 14.
2. John Adams, *Adams Family Correspondence* (L. H. Butterfield and Marc Friedlaender, editors; Harvard University Press, 1973), III: 342.
3. Robert Nozick, *Anarchy, State and Utopia* (Basic Books, 1974), p. xii.

Acknowledgments

The publisher of this work, The Foundation for Economic Education, has provided encouragement of and a literary outlet for a third of my writing, from 1981 to the present. I am deeply grateful on both accounts to the Foundation and to the editors of *The Freeman* with whom I have enjoyed a close, working relationship: Dr. Paul L. Poirot, the Reverend Edmund A. Opitz, Charles Hamilton, Brian Summers, and Dr. John W. Robbins. I have learned from each. My thanks also to Beth Hoffman for her superb job in editing this manuscript for publication, and to Mary Ann Murphy for her rapid, accurate typing.

My appreciation of the President of the Foundation, Dr. Hans F. Sennholz, for his invitation to collect my essays in this volume knows no bound.

My family and friends have given me their support throughout the years and it is hardly necessary to say and obvious once said that I could never have produced so many fine essays, let alone a collection, without them.

To my mother and father, in particular, I owe everything and with love and respect I am proud to dedicate this work to them.

I would also like to acknowledge the place of first publication of the essays that have been edited into the chapters of this book. Chapter I-1 is adapted from "Libertarian Sympathies: Heart and Mind," *The Freeman 38(March 1988):103–105*. Chapter I-2 is adapted from "Liberty and Property," *The Freeman 37(May 1987): 175–178*. Chapter I-3 is adapted from "Productive Advances: Who Benefits Most?" *The Freeman 37(July 1987): 251*. Chapter I-4 is based on "Civilization," *The*

Freeman 38(November 1988): 419. Chapter I-5 is based on "Economic Power," *The Freeman 38(February 1988): 64–65,* "Pure Socialism," *The Freeman 39(January 1989): 3,* and "Myths of the Rich Man," *The Freeman 39(February 1989): 82–83*. Chapter I-6 is adapted from "The New Bondage," *The Freeman 32(April 1982): 243–248,* which, in turn, was based on a letter to *The New York Times* (August 2, 1981). Chapter I-7 is based on a review of George F. Will's *The Pursuit of Virtue and Other Tory Notions* which appeared in *The Freeman 32(October 1982): 638–640*. Chapter I-8 is adapted from "America at Her Best," *The Freeman 31(November 1981): 667–670*. Chapter I-9 is adapted from "Declarative Law," *The Freeman 35(November 1985): 684–687*. Chapter I-10 is based on "Product Information on the Market," *The Freeman 36(January 1986): 29–33* and "Dimensions of Competition," *The Freeman 38(June 1988): 212–215*. Chapter II-1 is adapted from Joseph S. Fulda and Patrick J. Vincent, "Are There Too Many Lawyers?" *The Freeman 43(January 1993): 19–20*. Chapter II-2 is adapted from "Liberties Lost in the Balance," *The Freeman 36(May 1986): 164–165*. Chapter II-4 is adapted from "'Corrective' State Action," *The University Bookman 29(1989): (2)31–33*. Chapter II-5 is adapted from "Pay Television and Property Rights," *The Freeman 37(June 1987): 220–222*. Chapter II-6 is adapted from "The Market and Scarce Resources," *The Freeman 34(August 1984): 497*. Chapter II-7 is adapted from "Standard Textbooks: Who Decides?" *Measure 100(November 1991): 9*. Chapter II-8 is adapted from "Government and Merit in the Universities," *The University Bookman 27(Fall 1986): (1)14–15*. Chapter II-9 is adapted from "Campus Activities: Who Pays the Bills?" *The Freeman 38(May 1988): 200–201*. Chapter II-10 is adapted from "Paradoxical Taxi Fares," *The Freeman 38(July 1988): 286*. Chapter II-11 is adapted from "Profit Motive Works Around Clock in Manhattan to House Homeless," *Free Press Herald* of Canton, Ohio (May 9, 1990). Chapter II-12 is adapted from "The

Moral Case for a Balanced Budget," *The Freeman 37(March 1987): 90*. Chapter III-2 is adapted from "Scandals," *The Freeman 37 (December 1987): 444–446*. Chapter III-3 is adapted from "Congressional Reforms," *The Freeman 43(March 1983): 83*. Chapter III-4 is adapted from "The Appearance of Impropriety," *Spectrum 3(Spring/Summer 1988): 31–32*.

Table of Contents

III. Narrow Ethics

I. FOUNDATIONS of LIBERTARIANISM

1

Libertarian Sympathies: Heart and Mind

[N]o free government, or the blessings of liberty, can be preserved to any people, but ... by frequent recurrence to fundamental principles.

—Virginia Bill of Rights[1]

Two questions invariably asked of me by those unacquainted with libertarian thought and surprised at many of the observations and arguments I put forth are "Why are you so committed a libertarian?" and "Given the appeal of the freedom philosophy, why should it have so few adherents?"

This essay, then, is my attempt to answer these questions about the attractions of the philosophy that so many of us have embraced, and so many more have yet to embrace.

Libertarianism appeals to both heart and mind. For many of us, especially the young, libertarianism arises as a natural consequence of a free-spirited personality: yearning to enjoy life, with as few encumbrances as possible, and to answer to no one but ourselves and (for some of us) God.

For many of us, also, libertarianism arises from deep-seated philosophical convictions about the nature and dignity of man and the way the world works. These convictions are variations on three themes.

The first is the spiritual case for liberty: that men are naturally born with free will and that it is, therefore, both their right and their duty—their unique destiny—to use this God-given capacity to choose among alternatives,[2] for good or for bad, for happiness or for unhappiness—provided, of course, that in so doing they in no way remove the free will of others.

The second is the moral case for liberty: that the use of

force, except in self-defense—individual or collective—is simply wrong. This understanding of the inviolable nature of the rights of man arises directly from a conception of his dignity.

The third is the empirical case for liberty: that a free society promises the greatest good of the greatest number, that freedom truly works. Unlike the spiritual and moral premises, which to many are self-evident, the way the marketplace works to our benefit is often subtle. It is, for example, not obvious that the benefits of productive advances are greatest for the poor,[3] that distribution-of-income figures do *not* show a permanent underclass in capitalist society,[4] that we benefit most from the liberty of *others* and in ways we can barely imagine,[5] that government programs are *necessarily* wasteful,[6] that the market is *self*-regulating if given the chance,[7] and that the beneficiaries of state action are usually visible and well-organized, while those who lose as a result of state action are usually so diffuse a group as to make it difficult and unprofitable to organize and gain visibility.[8]

Because of these and other subtleties, it is usually necessary for those who espouse the freedom philosophy to make a separate, empirical case against each existing or proposed government program or regulation. This can be not only frustrating, but also particularly difficult for functions government assumed long ago, because it is hard to know just how the market—co-ordinating the spontaneous responses of many millions of people—would today handle these functions. Thus a grounding in economic history, as well as in economic theory, is needed to provide much of the empirical case for private schools, privately owned streets, voluntary charity and relief, privately provided economic security, privately coined money, and the like.

Nevertheless, given enough such examples, the individualist convinced of both the spiritual and moral case for liberty will accept the empirical case as well. In so doing, he will add to the claim that liberty is a virtue, the further claim that liberty is a blessing that promotes human happiness. These three philosophical themes taken together both support and are supported by the primal appeal of freedom that is basic to so much of our personalities.

There is a great danger, though, when the primal appeal of liberty is not accompanied by philosophical conviction. For then the temptation arises to use government to expand liberty, rather than to destroy it. Of course, the use of force cannot—by definition—expand liberty, but there are a great many with libertarian sympathies, perhaps including most Americans, but without a sufficient grounding in theory, who think that it can. We might call them social libertarians and their idea, oxymoronic as it is, socialized libertarianism.

To them, as to Lord Acton and philosopher-economist John Stuart Mill, liberty means freedom not just from coercion, but also from the opinions, customs, and traditions of the many. To gain such freedom from the valuation of others, a social libertarian may well be tempted to advocate state coercion not seeing, for the moment, that, as Hayek so beautifully expounds in *The Constitution of Liberty,* the empirical case for freedom holds true of the very opinions, customs, and tradition he feels (but is not coercively) bound by.[9] In any case, state action violates the spiritual and moral constraints on coercion the social libertarian normally accepts.

This blind spot is particularly notable and noticeable in the case of invidious discrimination against members of a minority group. Even those who normally make a very strong case for the freedoms of association (which include the freedom not to associate) and the right to privacy (which includes the right to scrutiny-free relationships) are tempted to make a major exception where invidious discrimination is concerned.[10] The philosophical libertarian, in contrast, distinguishes carefully between persecution and discrimination and while prohibiting the former with all the force of the law and the state, leaves the latter subject to moral opprobrium by the citizenry and to the powerful rectifying institutions of the marketplace.[11]

Social libertarians also might advocate that employers not be allowed to test employees for drugs or truthfulness and that landlords not be allowed to prohibit cohabitation, children, pets, or washing machines. For in each case, although freedom of choice is clearly contracted, the choices available to the advocates of state action have equally clearly been substantially expanded, albeit at the expense of those whose freedom of choice has been contracted. This point is one which causes some discomfort for the proponent of liberty, for it is undoubtedly true that in many instances we are prevented from acting as we like or required to act in ways we do not like, even though no coercion is involved. Yet both the employer's terms and the landlord's terms, as irrational, onerous, or even immoral as they may be, and as little as we may wish to defend them, are tacitly accepted by the employee and the tenant in staying on his job and in his domicile. What social libertarians would do, in essence, is replace the criterion of liberty with one of reasonableness. If there are not good and sufficient reasons for the conditions attached to the job or the tenancy, they advocate that those conditions must not be allowed to stand.

Furthermore, social libertarians argue, if socialized libertarianism is rejected on the grounds that continuance in a position is tacit acceptance, why not try the principle one step further and respond that the coercive powers of the state are also tacitly accepted by anyone continuing to live within its borders?

If there is a weakness with philosophical libertarianism, the social libertarian continues, it is the narrowness of the definition of coercion. In their view, the employer and the landlord do exercise a form of coercion and one which is best prevented by coercion from the state.[12]

These are serious objections which must be answered and which present difficulties for anyone who has ever held a job or a tenancy with unreasonable conditions—and who among us has not? The best answer to these misgivings is a simple question. "Unreasonable to whom?" Or, "Reasons not thought good and sufficient by whom?" Obviously not to the employer or landlord whose liberty it is proposed to limit and whose property it is proposed to regulate. Furthermore, if the employer or landlord *is* wrong about the reasonableness of his conditions, the market will exact penalties in higher salaries, lower rents, and the like.[13]

Moreover, such an analysis does not even consider all the harmful side effects of the state's entering the picture, including the potential for the state to become the final arbiter of what constitutes good and sufficient reasons and what is or is not reasonable, thus placing the housing and employment sectors under the control of the state, a near-inevitable outcome that a social libertarian would surely deplore.[14]

Finally, the tacit acceptance of a property owner's conditions—whether the ownership is of a corporation or rental housing—is not akin to the state's claim over its resident citizens. The state does have sovereignty—a monopoly on the retaliatory use of force within its borders—but it lacks, or should lack, ownership—a monopoly on the control and use of the property within its borders. Ownership arises by what philosopher Robert Nozick has called "the entitlement theory,"[15] which dates back to John Locke.[16] Sovereignty does not properly confer ownership, and in those polities where it *is* taken to include ownership, there is and can be no liberty.[17] And that is a tragedy which should convince the social libertarian to acquire a taste for philosophical libertarianism and, despite the temptation, not to compromise so sacred a principle as liberty—freedom from coercion—for an expanded notion of freedom that must diminish the very liberty in whose name it is promoted.

1. The Virginia Bill of Rights, *Sources of Our Liberties* (Richard Perry, editor; American Bar Foundation, 1959), p. 312.

2. See *Deuteronomy 30:19*.

3. See I-3, below.

4. See, for example, George Gilder, "The Economy of Frustration," *Wealth and Poverty* (Basic Books, 1981), pp. 19–20.

5. See, for example, F. A. Hayek, "Freedom as Opportunity for the Unknown Few," *The Constitution of Liberty* (Gateway Editions, 1972), Chapter 2, section 5, pp. 30–32.

6. See, for example, Milton Friedman and Rose Friedman, *Free to Choose* (Harcourt Brace Jovanovich, 1980), pp. 115–119.

7. See, for example, I-10 and II-6, below.

8. The classical example here is the tariff, although the principle holds true for virtually all government interventions.

9. F. A. Hayek, "Custom and Tradition," *The Constitution of Liberty* (Gateway Editions, 1972), Chapter 4, especially section 5, pp. 61–62.

10. For a definitive statement of this, see George Will, *Statecraft as Soulcraft* (Simon and Schuster, 1983), pp. 86–87.

11. See, for example, Milton Friedman, "Capitalism and Discrimination," *Capitalism and Freedom* (University of Chicago Press, 1962), pp. 108–118.

12. F. A. Hayek deals with this stubborn issue head-on in "Coercion and the State," *The Constitution of Liberty* (Gateway Editions, 1972), Chapter 9, pp. 133–147. Hayek's discussion is essential for the philosophical libertarian troubled by defining liberty as the absence of coercion.

13. See footnote 11.

14. As an example of this usurpation, the state now regularly decides whether, and to what extent, gender is a relevant and reasonable criterion in social and economic activity.

15. Robert Nozick, "The Entitlement Theory," *Anarchy, State and Utopia* (Basic Books, 1974), pp. 150–153.

16. John Locke, "Of Property," *Two Treatises of Government* (Peter Laslett, editor; Cambridge University Press, 1967), II: 5: 25–51.

17. See, for example, I-2, below.

2

Liberty and Property: Connections

> *[A]s a man is said to have a right to his property, he may be equally said to have a property in his rights.*
>
> —James Madison[1]

Perhaps the best way to illumine the connection between the economics and philosophy of liberty is to uncover the relationship between liberty and property.

There is no more authentically conservative idea than the rights of property. What is less understood is that there is no more authentically liberal idea either. The alliance between liberty and property is nowhere more celebrated than in John Locke's second treatise of government, *An Essay Concerning the True Original, Extent, and End of Civil Government,* and it is to the master that we turn for its exposition.

To Locke, property was a broad concept. Anything that one has a right to is his property, for rights are proprietary interests, no more, no less. Indeed Locke often interchanges "property" and "rights." Everything we have is thus a property: life, limb, health, reputation, and possessions. Thus broadly must be understood Locke's noble statement, oft cited but little understood, "Government has no other end but the preservation of property."[2] So he explains himself, to anyone who troubles to look.

It is "lives, liberties, and estates, which," Locke informs his readers, "I call by the general name, *property*."[3] Earlier he had written, "Every man has a property in his own person. This nobody has any right to but himself. The labour of his body, and the work of his hands, we may say, are properly his."[4] Properly his—or proper to him—because man has "in himself the great foundation of property."[5] Again and again, this unifying idea—property, or rights—lends simplicity and beauty to this earliest exposition of limited government.

We have, for example, a proprietary interest in our children which though it gives us the exclusive right to rear them is neither unlimited nor permanent: We have created an equal with rights of his own. The moral basis of religion is much the same: "For men being all the workmanship of one omnipotent, and infinitely wise Maker . . . they are his property, whose workmanship they are . . . ."[6] Whether the relation between God and man is master-slave or father-child is the subject of many a theological discourse and an endless dialogue between Creator and created. Marriage is also a proprietary interest as it "consist[s] chiefly in such a communion and right in one another's body . . . ."[7] The commitments of contract, founded on mutual considerations, are also proprietary interests, rights to be secured by the law of the land.

Richard Baxter, an English divine contemporary with Locke, summed it up this way: "Every man is born with a propriety in his own members, and nature giveth him a propriety in his children, and his food and other just acquisitions of his industry . . . . And men's lives and liberties are the chief parts of their propriety."[8] Perhaps more than anything else, it is Locke's broad, underlying conception of property that makes his *magnum opus* cohere so gracefully.

It also illuminates the connection between liberty and property. Liberty, after all, refers to the *absence* of coercion. It is thus a condition of noninterference with one's properties, one's proprietary interests, one's rights: noninterference with one's person, family, worship, contracts, and possessions. That is liberty and it is of property. Jefferson's statement that governments were instituted to secure the rights of man is Locke's assertion that governments exist for the preservation of property recast in the language of a later time.

The preservation of attachments, of man to God, of family

ties, of contractual commitments, of a man to his life, fortune, and honor is perhaps the essence of conservatism rightly understood. The closely allied classical liberal tradition is about freedom: the freedom to attach, the freedom not to attach, the freedom not to be interfered with in one's attachments. Government is ever a threat to such freedom and attachment, to liberty and property, for it has within its means the dread taxing power. If we understand property broadly as did Locke, then the power to tax—to take property—is readily seen to encompass all the multifarious interventions of the state in our lives. The power to tax is indeed the power to destroy.

Such an understanding of property and taxation gives the lie to those who incessantly call for "national service" and their fond belief that this would lower taxes. Of course, it would simply make the state's consumption of the energies of the citizenry more direct and more coercive, shifting the burden of taxation from "that property which men have in their . . . goods" to "that property which men have in their persons."[9] As George Gilder has written, the shift is regressive, "the Moloch of the closing circle": "The rates of taxation climb and the levels of capital decline, until the only remaining wealth beyond the reach of the regime is the very protein of human flesh, and that too is finally taxed, bound, and gagged, and brought to the colossal temple of the state—a final sacrifice of carnal revenue to feed the declining elite. This is the destination of all dictatorship . . . ."[10]

But what of that property which men have in their goods and in their land? How do rights in places and things preserve liberty? The answer lies more in the nature of human action than in the nature of places and things. Human action not only engages our persons; most action is performed on, with, or by the agency of property. And all human action takes place on the Good Earth, where by the grace of God man has erected his civilization. Thus is liberty of property and thus does the preservation of property rights secure liberty. The

Founders did not have available the comprehensive and beautiful vision of human action and economic freedom that we owe to the Austrian school, but this simple insight, that liberty is largely of property, never left them for a moment. That is why the polity they constructed so protected property and why their hope for freedom was realized here for so long, so well.

To come to a full appreciation of the role of personal property in human action, consider the dearth of activities that would remain were all private (non-state-sanctioned) uses of personal property suddenly banned. Trade and enterprise would vanish, just as Marx, who worked for the abolition of private property, wished. Universities, broadcasters, and printers would have to close up shop, and everything else would soon follow. Indeed only three activities seem to be left to us: disorderly fistfighting (neither gloves, a whistle, nor a ring is allowed), yelling at large crowds (yelling because microphones are property; the crowd is gathered because radio, television, and other means of telecommunication involve property), and making love in the grass (beds being property). There was a time when this was largely what was meant by freedom: the reader may recall this as the Freedom of the Sixties. It is what is left of freedom when we are free to use our persons as we wish, but not our property. It is without question a caricature of freedom.

But even such skeletal personal freedom assumes the right to use the land as one wishes. Without such property rights, even these meager liberties are preserved only as long as the state pretermits. Land use regulations become ever more proscriptive and ever more prescriptive until one finds oneself utterly without choice of how to live on the land: The condition is known as serfdom and it is the logical extension of land use regulations and the actual unfortunate lot of millions.

When the territory of the free society—the many arenas of private activity—is not respected, the liberties of its denizens are woefully insecure. That is why state control of land, its use, and its distribution has been so prominent a feature of socialist programmes, and why such miserable and blatant failures as collectivist agriculture generated enthusiasm among the ruling elite, long, long after being thoroughly discredited. These leaders understood full well—as did their predecessors in other closed societies, feudal societies, for instance—that the private domains of a free society powerfully circumscribe the long arm and reach of the state. Private property is thus for them a thing to be greatly feared.

Concern for the security of real property is not new to the tradition of liberty. Indeed it is one of the principal concerns of the *Magna Carta* and eventually made its way into our Bill of Rights as part of the third, fourth, and fifth amendments to the federal constitution.

Let us move forward in time and examine the liberty-property connection as it is manifested today. Indeed today much abridgment of liberty comes under the guise of regulation of property, both real and personal. Whether the state draws the line around the object the man wishes to use or around the man who wishes to use the object is only a matter of perspective. What results is a contraction of choice, a limitation of the field of possibilities for human action, in short an abridgment of liberty.

Regulations on farms and farm products inflate the costs of production and abridge the farmer's liberty to produce. Urban zoning ordinances abridge the associative freedoms and erect barriers to commerce, enterprise, and peaceful residence. Airwaves, too, are real property. When their use is circumscribed by "fairness," political access, public access, equal time, community service, and public interest requirements, it is the liberty of expression that is violated, in particular the liberty not to speak. When labeling requirements are placed on substances, it is the same freedom that is diminished along with the freedom of enterprise.

Productive human action is greatly encumbered by detailed regulations on capital goods and plant by the likes of OSHA and USDA, on transportation by the likes of DOT, FAA, and NHTSA, and on housing by HUD and countless state, county, and municipal agencies. The demands of these agencies are on people, not on machines, trucks, and houses. It is people who are directed to associate with such and such a person in the name of fairness, to transport only such and such an item in the name of fair competition, and to build machines in this or that way in the name of worker safety.

But it is precisely because control over people is being exerted through control of property that such measures can never meet their goals. Writes William E. Simon:

> The common feature of OSHA regs, EPA "zero discharge" crusades, and NHTSA efforts to improve traffic safety is that they seek to create a risk-free existence by manipulating objects. But most accidents and other health and safety hazards . . . result from human error or carelessness. The crusade to create a totally risk-free environment is therefore doomed to failure from the outset.[11]

Empirical evidence supporting this generality and demonstrating the incredible lack of cost-effectiveness in what is known as the "command and control" method of regulation has become increasingly acknowledged in recent years.

The connection between liberty and private property can be further illumined by an examination of the connection between their polar opposites: totalitarianism and the abolition of private property. "The theory of the Communists may be summed up in the single sentence: Abolition of private property," wrote Marx.[12] Lenin was later to write: "The scientific concept of the dictatorship [of the proletariat] means nothing other than unlimited government unrestrained by any laws or any absolute rules and supporting itself by force."[13] The connection between the aim of the former and the reality of the latter is evinced by a consideration of Marx's central proposals: placing under state control the instruments of production (farms and factories), the means of association (transportation and communication), and the sources of ideas (schools, universities, churches, printing presses, and other media).

Broadly considered, the old adage is quite right: We are what we consume. The foods we eat, clothing we wear, houses in which we dwell, furnishings with which we decorate them, appliances we use, haircuts we get, discussions into which we enter, places we visit, books we read, pictures we watch, courses of study on which we embark, ideas to which we adhere, and the God we worship: these are all the things that make us what we are: they *are* our civilization.

Control over everything consumed, from agricultural products and manufactured goods to the company of others and the ideas of the day, is thus the power to shape civilization. Marx instinctively reaches for the throat of the free society when he suggests state control of the means of production. "The means of production," after all, is a prosaic phrase. We are talking of nothing less than the source of supply, the means of satisfying human needs and wants. Granting the state power over this satisfaction does more than place every man in "terror of effective deprival . . . of his business and his livelihood,"[14] although it does that: It allows the state to define society.

The relation between Marxism and the more virulent Leninism thus has a simple, syllogistic structure: We are, broadly speaking, what we consume. In a planned economy, what is produced determines what is consumed. Therefore, control over what is produced determines the nature of our lives. In a market economy, in contrast, what we would consume is all that can be produced. Control over what is produced—and over what is consumed—is left in the hands of the common folk, you and me: That is the essence of a free society.

1. James Madison, *Letters and Other Writings of James Madison* (R. Worthington, 1884), IV: 478.

2. John Locke, *Two Treatises of Government* (Peter Laslett, editor; Cambridge University Press, 1967), II: 94.

3. *Ibid.*, II: 123.

4. *Ibid.*, II: 27.

5. *Ibid.*, II: 44.

6. *Ibid.*, II: 6.

7. *Ibid.*, II: 78.

8. Richard Baxter, *The Second Part of the Nonconformist's Plea for Peace* (Printed for John Hancock at the three Bibles near the Royal Exchange in Cornhil, 1680), pp. 54–55.

9. John Locke, *op cit.*, II: 173.

10. George Gilder, *Wealth and Poverty* (Basic Books, 1981), p. 258.

11. William Simon, *A Time for Action* (Berkley Books, 1980), p. 89.

12. Karl Marx and Frederick Engels, *The Communist Manifesto* (Samuel Moore, translator; New York Labor News Company, 1948), p. 25.

13. Quoted in Lance Morrow, "What Workers Get out of Communism," *Time* 116: 11, September 15, 1980, p. 102.

14. Herbert Hoover, *The Challenge to Liberty* (Charles Scribner's Sons, 1934), p. 82.

3

The Rising Tide of Productive Advances: The Market and the Poor

The free enterprise system allows inventors and investors to reap the rewards of creativity and risk. But in a market economy, those who gain *most* from the productive advances conceived and designed by inventors and funded by investors are the poor.

Let us examine several productive advances and see to whom the benefits accrue. Consider first the printing press. The very rich had scribes and private secretaries to do their clerical work, but the very poor are now literate in numbers once deemed impossible. Or to move up the centuries, consider the television. The rich had hours of leisure and the funds for private entertainment to fill them. The poor, however, now have an entertainment cornucopia undreamt of in earlier ages. As a third example, consider air travel. The rich were able to afford weeks of travel by land or sea, while their properties continued to generate income. Those less well off, on the other hand, would never see distant lands or relations without air travel. Or consider antibiotics, one of the twentieth century's miracles. The rich who live in sanitary, spacious quarters have had less need of these wonder drugs than those who occupy crowded, unsanitary slum areas. Finally, consider that mundane appliance, the vacuum cleaner. The rich often have others do their housekeeping. Their housekeepers, in contrast, have had their jobs simplified and their hourly output increased by the vacuum cleaner's invention.

From little things to big things, the principle holds. Productive advances help everyone, but most of all the less well-to-do.

This is hardly limited to inventions and discoveries, but applies to improvements in productive methods as well. Who has been helped the most by specialization, mass production, automation, and robotics? The rich consumer could always afford the work of the skilled craftsman, but the ordinary shopper depends on the economies of modern technology and productive methods for the wide variety of household items from which he chooses. Likewise, advances in these productive methods may enrich the factory owner, but it is his workers whose jobs over the decades have become lighter, more meaningful, and better paid. Nor is this observation true only of blue-collar workers. From the pencil to the typewriter to the electric typewriter to the word processor, the jobs of the lowest-paid, white-collar workers have also become lighter, more meaningful, and better paid.

Nor have all these advances thrust millions into idleness—although there is always some transitional but transitory dislocation—as the doomsayers have long warned. Rather, mankind's energies have been channeled more and more into the good things of life and less and less into its bare necessities.

Government redistribution of wealth has not been the cause of the remarkable improvement in our standard of living over the years. Only productive advances make the same physical effort count for more and more and only economic growth so arising can truly increase everyone's rewards. And when productivity is enhanced and the economy grows, it is the poor who are lifted most by the rising tide.

4

"Civilization": A Word of Commerce, Not Virtue

[T]he sphere of an all-pervading commerce . . . daily diffusing over its surface the light and blessings of civilization.

—John C. Calhoun[1]

The Declaration of Independence lists "the pursuit of happiness" as among the most fundamental of rights. In this the framers were realists, rather than moralists.

Jefferson spoke of the "march of civilization" as "a cloud of light, increasing our knowledge and improving our condition."[2] And, indeed, civilization has greatly advanced in both material wealth and its intellectual underpinnings: Steadily, clearly, and progressively the standard of living has risen and the proportion of total output dedicated to life's necessities has fallen. Indeed, in many cases, today's understanding of a necessity was yesterday's understanding of a luxury.

But although moralists may prefer to think of civilization as progress in "the pursuit of virtue," evidence for this is scanty. Violence, coercion, and fraud flourish everywhere, even in the most "civilized" and "advanced" countries. The crimes and sins of man against man are no less abundant now than in yesteryear. And, no one can deny that this century has seen more naked evil than all of previous history considered together.

To be "civilized" means, literally, to be "fit for life in cities." And indeed it is the cities that are most vibrant economically and intellectually, centers of commerce and know-how, filled with trade and economic and intellectual specialization and co-operation. It was Emerson who declared: "The test of civilization is the power of drawing the most benefit out of cities."[3]

As Jefferson also predicted, however, cities are among the places least given to virtue and most given to vice, with violence done to persons and property everywhere in sight.

So what does this mean for those of us dedicated to the cause of liberty? I think it means that while the pursuit of happiness, and the economic and intellectual progress that makes it possible, is aided greatly by the co-operation, competition, and specialization of the marketplace as exemplified by great cities, the pursuit of virtue is intrinsically a matter of individual effort directed inwards.

---

1. John C. Calhoun, *Disquisition on Government* in *Calhoun: Basic Documents* (John Anderson, editor; Bald Eagle, 1952), p. 84.

2. Thomas Jefferson, *The Jeffersonian Cyclopedia* (John Foley, editor; Funk and Wagnalls Company, 1900), p. 145.

3. Attributed to Ralph Waldo Emerson by *The Home Book of Quotations* (10th edition; Burton Stevenson, editor; Dodd Mead and Company, 1967), p. 277.

5

Economic Power: A Socialist Myth

Economic power is a recurring theme among political theorists ranging from radical political economist John Kenneth Galbraith on the left to neoconservative intellectual Irving Kristol on the right. The doctrine that wealth is power is almost never challenged in our day and in many rather subtle ways has come to underlie much public policy: Public campaign financing, campaign contribution limitations, equal time, antitrust laws, and estate taxes are examples. This concept, which originated in the late nineteenth century[1] and has since lain dormant in the public mind, needs re-examination.

Any analysis of economic power must begin with a clear conception of power and its antithesis, liberty. Power, as I understand it, is the capacity to rule others: to make decisions for them without their consent and, in particular, to allocate their time and direct their energies. Liberty, in contrast, is a condition of non-interference and self-rule in which people are free to make decisions for themselves and in which they apportion their time and channel their energies in such manner as to them seems most satisfying.

If the capacity to coerce is the sum of power, it is hard to see how it inheres in a pile of riches. The usual reply is that wealth can be used to obtain instruments of coercion along with those willing to use them, and that power can indeed be found in a stockpile of weapons and men of violence. Now this is all very true, but inasmuch as the unholy alliance between wealth and force, public (e.g., bribery) and private (e.g., organized crime), is universally proscribed in free republics, it cannot account for the tirades, so common in the media, against economic power. Economic power in that sense has no apologists and, therefore, no detractors.

Nor is it the holders of power, as we have defined it, who stand accused of its use in the economic realm. Indeed, government is seen as the enemy of economic power, Galbraith's "countervailing power," the embodiment of Kristol's populist temper. Government may indeed tax, subsidize, regulate, and monopolize, but it is rather the wealthy and the corporations who are said to enjoy economic power. But the only power which properly attends on wealth alone is ***dominium***: the "complete power to use, to enjoy, and to dispose of property at will."[2] But is this power? That is, is it control over one's own domain (liberty) or control over the domain of others (power)? Far from being a power, dominium is a liberty, specifically the liberty to do with the fruits of one's labor and the return on one's investment as one wills.

Thus, proponents of the concept of economic power must be referring to something other than power over the economy. What they mean, in fact, by "economic power" is the ability to influence a variety of social and economic conditions through the use of one's wealth in a volitive, rather than coercive, manner. In a market society, those with the most "purchasing power" ultimately decide what will be produced, in greater measure than will those with less purchasing power. Likewise, those with the most to invest will proximately decide what goods will be produced and what services will be offered, in greater measure than will those with less to invest.

Yet this influence over the free economy is central to its operation: Either what is produced will determine what can be consumed, as in the command economy, or what will be consumed determines what can be produced, as in the market economy. Likewise, either profits and losses will take capital from those not satisfying consumer wishes and reward those more sensitive to others' needs, or capital will be allocated and production decisions will be made in accordance with political, rather than economic, criteria.

The notion of economic power, then, is really nothing other than what an honest socialist would admit is economic freedom, what Marx called "that single, unconscionable freedom."[3] This freedom, mistakenly labeled "power," is often resented when it comes to play in the political sphere, and leads to all manner of election "reforms." It is also resented in the economic sphere, and leads to a variety of anti-competitive regulatory "reforms." It is perhaps most resented in the social sphere—just remember back to Mrs. Reagan's very difficult first months as First Lady—and leads to sweeping demands for a new social order.

What is really resented is the necessarily unequal nature of this influence that will always obtain when men are left free. The gurus of the far left denounce concentrations of wealth as power, because the resulting influence over who will lead and what will be produced and consumed is something they feel is best left to them and their plans for our future.

What other explanation can honestly be put forth for collectivist denunciations of wealth in capitalist society, in view of what has been their "solution" to the "problem" of concentrations of wealth. They have supported regimes which have combined all corporations into one giant Corporation, endowed it with all natural resources, armed it, invested it with legislative and judicial powers, granted it the police power, imbued it with quasi-spiritual authority, placed its public relations department in charge of the media and its acquisitions department in charge of the military and then, as final sublimating acts, replaced a much-decried self-perpetuating board of directors with a self-perpetuating Party elite and renamed this new Corporation, the State.

That has been the socialist prescription for concentrations of *both* wealth *and* power,[4] and, as we have learned, it is a very clear guarantee of poverty, misery, and tyranny, the three things alone which socialism has produced beyond comparison.

But while the resentment is both present and unmistakable, there is also more than a little fear of the concentrations of wealth in the hands of the rich, and insofar as this concern underlies a good deal of the talk of "economic power," even by ordinary people in ordinary conversation, it is well to treat it with some seriousness.

As an example of this, whenever privatization is contemplated for such necessaries as potable water or the streets, the discussion is clouded by fear of what "the rich man" who provides the resource might or might not do. The rich man might acquire all the drinking water and let no one else drink, or all the streets and let no one emerge from his home. Or the rich man might charge a small fortune for a glass of water or an afternoon walk on the streets, with none to stop him, since he is the owner. The rich man, it is further feared, might provide no water and build no streets. If the state does not provide for us by marketing these necessaries, perhaps no one will, and society will perish.

These fears are little more than myths. After all, there are plenty of other things we need—food, clothing, shelter—and yet none of the fears people have of the rich have materialized in any free market system. Society is not at the mercy of the malevolent rich man controlling its necessaries. A man who holds vast reservoirs of water or large parcels of land and makes no economic use of it out of spite (and it is fear of spitefulness that is behind this myth) will soon find the management costs of his properties causing him to lose them. The water will lose its potability, the pipes will become rusty, and the whole system will become worthless; the streets will fall into disrepair and require endless reconstruction while earning no income. Certainly, that is not how the rich man has acquired his wealth!

But, still, what if? All that will happen is that large holdings of real estate will be converted to streets and reservoirs by others, rich or poor. As long as free entry—competition—is allowed, the rich man who owns necessaries and will not market them spites only himself, and he will lose his fortune. Someone else will see the need, convert his property to the now-more-marketable use and take the rich man's erstwhile profits away.

Nor can the rich man buy up all the streets or reservoirs and charge arbitrarily large sums for these necessaries. As he raises the price, conversion of other resources to these purposes becomes increasingly attractive. And, substitutes, once far too expensive even to be contemplated let alone developed, begin to become attractive as well. All it takes is one person with a vision—be he rich or poor—and the consumer demand for a water-substitute or a street-substitute will be satisfied. As Julian Simon demonstrated in *The Ultimate Resource,*[5] the human mind, throughout history, has always been able to find alternatives which satisfy the very same need as some resource once thought to be indispensable.

Finally, we must remark that the situation itself—a malevolent rich man monopolizing all but providing nothing, or providing only at impossibly steep prices—is most artificial. Empirical studies have shown that as capitalist society progresses, the distribution of resources and the funds for capital investment tend to become more diffuse and mobile.[6] It is doubtful on both psychological and economic grounds whether (without state grants of monopoly power or the equivalent) the scenarios that underlie the myth of the malevolent, monopolizing rich man could ever come to pass. But the freedom-lover may rest assured that even if such concentrations of wealth and malice somehow did occur, all that would happen is that an adjustment would be made as natural resources, capital, labor, and entrepreneurial talent would be redistributed and re-allocated to meet the public's need, with special rewards to those who would turn the situation into an opportunity to provide and thus be provided for.

Nor does society, to consider the opposite fear, depend on the beneficence of the rich man to provide its necessaries. Were none of the rich interested in providing water or streets, the poor aspiring to become rich would provide, although perhaps not in large quantities mediated through big corporations.

Perhaps water would be sold by local vendors by the bucket. And, perhaps streets would be owned in small lots by the homeowners and shopkeepers on the block. Or, perhaps workers would acquire streets with their pension funds, an investment linked to the general economic performance of the area, much like today's pension funds consisting of stocks and bonds. I repeatedly say "perhaps," for no one can know just how the market arrangements for, say, water and streets would work out.

But work out they would—the price system guarantees it. As water and streets become scarcer and scarcer, their prices will rise in lockstep, and the opportunities for entrepreneurs become increasingly irresistible. In a society with an economy in which everyone is free to take advantage of the available opportunities, one need not worry about the do-nothing rich any more than the spiteful rich.

Again, of course, the situation is artificial. Those with the most capital acquired their riches by taking advantage of opportunities, not by ignoring them. But should they decline to invest their wealth in areas where human needs must be met, things will work out as new entrepreneurs replace the old rich and, again, exercise their resolve to provide and thus be provided for. As George Gilder has written, under the regime of the free market the Golden Rule is the principal law: One *must* provide to others, in order to be provided for himself.[7]

Under the alternative regime, the socialist model, this is not the case. Pure socialism, as defined by Marx, entails separate answers to the questions of production and consumption. The link between production and consumption in the free economy, namely that successful production provides the means and the only means for successful consumption, is to be abolished under the pure socialist regime. Instead of trading one's productive output for one's consumption, production is forced and consumption is free. No trade is necessary, for production is guaranteed by the coercive powers of the state (and later is voluntarily performed by selfless men in a utopia) and consumption becomes a basic human right.

Of course, pure socialism is so far from consonance with human nature that it has never been tried. There has never been a regime that has totally abolished exchange and money, as prescribed by Marx. This is because free consumption simply creates shortages of scarce goods, while forced production creates resentment, but not goods and services of quality. The endless variants of socialism that have been tried—and are still being tried in both the West and the East—while impure, partake of the ideas of forced production and free consumption, which is why they invariably fail. Only the free market, with consumption as the returns on production, can be guaranteed to provide for people's wants and needs, both amply and efficiently.

---

1. See Clarence Carson, *A Basic History of the United States: The Growth of America: 1878–1928 (Volume 4)* (American Textbook Committee, 1985), throughout.

2. *American College Dictionary* (Random House, 1970), p. 359.

3. Karl Marx and Frederick Engels, *The Communist Manifesto* (Samuel Moore, translator; New York Labor News Company, 1948), p. 11.

4. The joining of the state's coercive powers with wealth explains why socialism has often been referred to as state capitalism, however misleading the designation.

5. Julian Simon, *The Ultimate Resource* (Princeton University Press, 1981), throughout.

6. For a discussion of "the problem of diffusing ownership," see Louis Kelso and Mortimer Adler, *The Capitalist Manifesto* (Random House, 1958).

7. George Gilder, *Wealth and Poverty* (Basic Books, 1981), pp. 8, 9.

6

The Politics of Government Largesse

In a courageous address to the delegates of the NAACP convention, President Reagan spoke of "a new form of bondage" and offered blacks, as he did all Americans, a greater measure of economic liberty. *The New York Times* was quick to notice that the selfsame programs responsible for the new bondage formed the President's much-vaunted safety net. But there is no contradiction. The President was making a sensitive point about the nature of government nets. "One moment they're under you, the next moment they're on top of you," he was reminding us.

The realization that dependence on the state invariably leads to subservience to the state may come hard in nations whose democratic forms often lend themselves to a most mischievous conflation of government with society. But as Hamilton noted, "[P]ower over a man's subsistence amounts to a power over his will."[1] Such power is what Hoover meant when he wrote of "the terror of effective deprival to any man of his business and his livelihood."[2] These men understood that the dependence of free men and women on the state for their sustenance, what we might call the paradox of democratic socialism, would soon undermine the blessings of liberty in which they believed so fervently, each in his own way. It is in this context that the new bondage must be understood, for those to whom we give, as much as those from whom we take, are stripped of some of their dignity and personal freedom.

Let us examine the underpinnings of the new bondage. The annals of government intervention will show a decided propensity on the part of government to control what it does

Written in 1981, at the height of the Reagan ascendancy.

not support. Such diverse entities as local governments, business enterprises, private schools, and our lives come under this head. But rare indeed is the agency of the state which proffers support without demanding a measure of control. Nor has such control been found unconstitutional. As one judge wrote, "It is hardly lack of due process for the Government to regulate that which it subsidizes."[3] One can even argue, as Senator Barry Goldwater has, that the appropriation of tax monies ethically requires some regulation of their use.[4] Legally, ethically, and historically, then, subsidy and regulation have been inextricably intertwined. Such an observation, to be sure, is no argument for the regulation attendant upon subsidy, but rather an argument against subsidies in the first instance.

Examples of the subsidy-regulation nexus abound. New York City, the Chrysler Corporation, and the national endowments have each sacrificed something very dear to the American tradition in return for the financial blessings of the state: a tradition of self-government older than America herself, the autonomy of private enterprise, and artistic integrity.

Under the system of regulated subsidies, government has extended itself into all the nooks and crannies of heretofore private life: charity, education, medical care, agriculture, trade, production, scholarship, art, and family relations. The politics of in-kind welfare yield bizarre results. Thus, we tell our poor where to live—in housing segregated by social class—and how much to eat—and thus how much to weigh. We tell parents what their children must learn—the virtues of the state, the new morality, and our debt to ape-like creatures—and what they should eat for lunch. We tell our elderly what transportation to use and when to use it—malfunctioning state-run systems at odd hours. We decide what medical procedures to allow—unnecessary operations, for example—and when home care can be funded—when the President intercedes. We tell our farmers what crops are desirable—tobacco, for example—and what crops must be restricted—peanuts, for example. We tell our business community what merits encouragement—enterprises so forlorn as to attract no investors without subsidy—and what deserves discouragement—companies so successful that they can out-produce and undersell their competition. We fashion all these specifications and regulations as citizens of a democratic state; we must live under them as members of a free society.

But inasmuch as the decision to accept a subsidy is voluntary, can the regulation attendant upon it truly be thought inconsistent with the philosophy of liberty? The answer, I believe, is in the affirmative and for three reasons. First, we have already remarked on the tendency of the state to regulate that which it does not subsidize. Such regulations often arise from the proverbial transmutation of the carrot into the stick. All too often the real object of the state is not to subsidize what the politicians believe a worthwhile enterprise or endeavor, but to regulate what is still a free enterprise or a social endeavor, with the subsidy a choice means to that typical end. Thus, what begins as a condition for federal contracts may end as a condition for doing business with one's neighbor. What begins with subsidy as the reward for compliance with social goals may end with fines as the punishment for deviating from public policy. What begins when the state has not yet exhausted its resources and over-taxed its populace will remain long after the resources to support what has been taken over are gone.

It will be useful to contrast the regulated state subsidy with private employment or gifts granted in return for adherence to conditions established by the giver. The private employer cannot impose his conditions of employment on anyone who does not seek employment with him. The giver of gifts can withhold his largesse, but can impose no fines. The state, on the other hand, is ever ready to cross the sharp moral line which divides not giving from taking.

It is for this reason, too, that those concerned with the

growth of government should be wary of the state's assumption of additional functions, even if they are *completely* voluntary. Thus, even those government services or enterprises which are used only by those who so choose and which are completely funded by user fees are suspect. The Postal Service, after all, began with neither a monopoly nor a subsidy, but has long since acquired both. As long as the entity which owns and operates an enterprise is also the entity with coercive powers, what begins in freedom may end in compulsion.

A second objection to the regulation which attends subsidy is that the regulations issued often conflict with the rightful management of the tax monies involved. Thus racial guidelines for companies with government contracts, while voluntary, are an inefficient—not to mention immoral—use of public funds. Whether the contract is for sanitation or defense, it is best fulfilled without regard to social or political goals which misallocate resources.

Again, the contrast with the private sector is helpful. A private business may indeed set any conditions it desires for contractors who wish to do business with it, for it operates with its own funds, has no public trust, and will moreover likely be severely penalized by the market if it persists in operating by uneconomic criteria. The state's funding, on the other hand, is obtained not by mutual consent based on recognition of the efficient use of resources, but by that unilateral system of resource absorption known as taxation. Thus, a public trust to utilize funds economically arises.

Third, there comes the realization that acceptance of the subsidy is often not, after all, a full and free choice. Is the decision to send one's children to public school—to accept the state education subsidy—fully voluntary, or is the decision influenced by the forcible extraction of public school tuition monies via taxation? Not only does one have the sense that one has paid for the subsidy—that it is not a subsidy taken from others at all—one has been forcibly deprived of the resources to purchase the service on the market. State compulsory education laws leave no recourse, in the absence of such resources, but to patronize government schools.

Consider, as another example, our beleaguered automobile manufacturers. These once-successful giants have been saddled with a myriad of uneconomic regulations. Their ability to borrow funds for needed modernization has been hampered by incessant government issues. Their ability to use their own capital to modernize has been checked by a tax code biased against capital formation. Worst of all, for decades the demand for their product lines was distorted by an energy policy of price controls; the false signals which ensued led these overly trusting companies on down the road to ruination. After the state has thus crippled their ability to operate without subsidies, it beckons, privilege in hand: All it asks for in return is yet more control.

More often than not, the large, failing enterprises that government "saves" and ultimately runs are in need of saving only from the consequences of prior government interventions. Again, this is no argument for subsidies to such enterprises, but rather an argument against the controls accompanying such subsidies while they continue.

Likewise, the poor man will find his needs attended to by a host of paternalistic agencies offering in-kind benefits that drastically circumscribe consumer choice. Why is it that in this fair land populated by a generous people, private charity, which the chroniclers of voluntarism tell us was once plentiful, is no longer adequate? Government consumes a major portion of personal income, ostensibly for eleemosynary purposes, that is why. As Albert Jay Nock observed some sixty years ago, we are as likely to refer the man in need of aid to the appropriate government agency as to aid him ourselves. By absorbing such a large portion of our resources, Nock continued, government usurps social and interpersonal initiatives as well.[5] Indeed, it is no small tribute to the American character that so much that is worthy is still supported privately, without subsidy or favor, despite confiscatory taxation.

In sum, then, while the decision to accept a subsidy is not made under duress, a great many coercive elements impinge on it. The element of volition in the regulations which are the price of subsidy is part of the insidious and seductive nature of subsidies, not cause to disregard the President's warning.

Nor are the motive forces behind the new bondage entirely benign. In part, such programs as in-kind benefits, categorical grants, and regulated subsidies derive from a decidedly illiberal view of those being aided. That is the view that having failed at self-sufficient production, the poor are not able to direct their own consumption wisely either. It is the view that the State, with the aid of the professionals and social scientists who understand such things, must therefore "help" them plan their lives. It is likewise the view that those majorities which dare to differ from the national majority on such issues as education and curriculum, the balance between liberty and security, the balance between the free exercise of religion and the proscription of its establishment, or the primacy of freedom of association are not to be trusted with the customary full faith and credit. The farmers cannot farm, the traders cannot trade, and the manufacturers cannot manufacture as well as can the "experts" in and around government, proponents of this view seem to be saying.

To a greater extent, though, these programs are the natural result of a corrupted democracy, in which the liberties and properties of individuals, once believed inalienable are regularly put to the trial of a majority vote. The election of representatives by district rather than at large localizes their political base. Thus, social, economic, ethnic, religious, occupational, or other interest groups, which in a larger area would form insignificant minority factions, are able, separately or in coalition, to gain political control over the district. ("By a faction," wrote Madison in the tenth *Federalist* paper,[6] "I understand a number of citizens, whether amounting to a majority or a minority of the whole, who are united and actuated by some common impulse of passion, or of interest, adverse to the rights of other citizens, or to the permanent and aggregate interests of the community.") The factious spirit, further promoted by the hypostatization of groups so common in the political discourse of the day, is then reflected in the likes of quotas, entitlements, and class action suits.

The turmoil of factions, which are today known as special interest groups, is also largely responsible for the new bondage. In-kind welfare programs and categorical grants permit the easy identification, coagulation, and milking of these interest groups by politicians. Politicians, in turn, are easily swayed to commit ever-greater depredations on the public treasury by factions which form a substantial part of their support. Further, in-kind programs, categorical grants, and regulated subsidies are particularly amenable to the bureaucratic empire building against which Jefferson and Tocqueville warned. If a man would have power over the activities of society, he need search no further than these baited hooks.

In contrast, only the poor would benefit from a single cash grant program, not the bureaucrats whose fiefdoms would be swept away, not the milk producers or construction workers assured a market without the rigors of competition, not the educators paid wages exactable from government only. Only the localities would benefit from block grants, not the supervising federal agents, not the intermediating state agents, not the implementing local agents, nor again the natural constituencies of the many categories that the Congress has so painstakingly isolated over the years.

This should come as no surprise, for the system of unlimited democracy in the name of charity is in reality a system whereby some benefit from the failures, misfortunes, and dependency of others. When subsidies are granted without specification or regulation, only those subsidized benefit. That is why such subsidies so rarely emerge from the political process.

---

1. *The Federalist* (Jacob Cooke, editor; Wesleyan University Press, 1961), Alexander Hamilton, 79: 531.

2. Herbert Hoover, *The Challenge to Liberty* (Charles Scribner's Sons, 1934), p. 82.

3. Mr. Justice Jackson writing for the Court in *Wickard v. Filburn,* 317 U.S. 111 at 131.

4. Barry Goldwater, *The Conscience of a Conservative* (Victor Publishing Company, 1960), pp. 81–82.

5. Albert Jay Nock, *Our Enemy, The State* (Hallberg Publishing Corporation, 1983), p. 24.

6. *The Federalist* (Jacob Cooke, editor; Wesleyan University Press, 1961), James Madison, 10: 57.

7

The Tory Position

Whether one follows his twice-weekly columns, reads his biweekly essays, or enjoys his lively comments as a television panelist one cannot fail to be impressed with George Will's expressive abilities. No other contemporary columnist has quite his way with words or quite his ability to extract, in a thousand words or so, that which is "'inside' public matters: Not what is secret, but what is latent, the kernel of principle and other significance that exists, recognized or not, 'inside' events, policies, and manners."

Beyond this, Will is the pre-eminent American spokesman for the Tory position[1] and his collection of essays and columns, *The Pursuit of Virtue and Other Tory Notions,*[2] is truly a restorative for those with Tory sensibilities and "the understanding that education consists primarily of arguing from, not with, [one's] patrimony."

In more than sixscore finely fashioned, tightly reasoned pieces, two distinctly different Tory sensibilities emerge. The first is the conscience of the cultural conservative lamenting "the decline of almost everything since 1914," of "stained glass minds" which, not altogether unseriously, "mourn the passing of the thirteenth century: feudal codes, heraldic banners, serried ranks of bishops . . ."

This is Will at his best, Will the social critic, conveying his urgent concern that Americans not lose what he terms "social sympathy": "The ability to comprehend, however dimly, how other people [must] live." This is the Will who writes of the "impediments invisible to most of us" that "are strewn through the lives of the elderly, and can imprison them"—little

As advocated by George Will.

things, like a heavy elevator door. This is the Will who comments on the aggressive marketing of gambling: "Such advertising is apt to be especially effective, and cruel, among people whose tribulations make them susceptible to dreams of sudden relief . . ." This is the Will educated at Oxford ("like civilization, it is cumulative, complicated, old and densely packed") who reminds us that education "presupposes students who acknowledge their incompleteness and teachers who believe that the purpose of education is to put something into students rather than to let something—'self-expression'—out."

As a cultural conservative, Will is concerned with public as well as private virtue. Here he recounts a visit to West Point:

> When asked why they had chosen West Point, the cadets' responses tended to emphasize the matter-of-fact . . . The spirit of the age has done its dirty work, so they are bashful about saying what is obviously, splendidly true of most of them: they are moved by patriotic as well as personal considerations.

But there is a second Tory voice which makes itself heard in Will's pages, and it is political. We are told right at the start, for example, that since "social and cultural anxieties find their way onto a society's political agenda" it is well to use government as "an instrument of conservative values, tempering and directing social dynamism." Will believes, with much of the religious right, that the "nation's moral makeup is, today, soft wax on which national leadership can leave a long-lasting impress." Needless to say, this is not the classical liberal's view of the rightful role of the state, and Will has the intellectual integrity not to present it as such:

> The overriding aim of liberalism, properly understood, is the expansion of liberty . . . Conservatism,

> properly understood, rejects the idea of a single overriding aim. Real conservatism is about balancing many competing values . . . .

Well, *life* is about balancing competing values, but the liberal does not want such decisions made in the political realm (i.e., by such repositories of virtue as politicians and bureaucrats). Not all of us have the same values, similarly ordered, and it is thus that liberty is not only itself a value but also the means by which all other values are chosen. Will seems to forget that such choice is not only man's birthright, but his moral imperative and unique destiny.

But if Will does not see liberty as primary or as determinative of other values, there is a reason for this. To Will, "libertarian" is almost synonymous with "libertine." Conservatism, he writes, "always requires resistance to libertarianism because libertarianism is a recipe for the dissolution of public authority, social and religious traditions, and other restraints needed to prevent license . . ." To call oneself a "libertarian conservative"—as so many of us do—is, he asserts, as contradictory as "promiscuous celibate." But few libertarians are nihilists, and those who are never redeem themselves by adding to "libertarian" the noble label "conservative." Indeed, confusion is being promoted here at a rather elementary level: The doctrine that morality ought not to be imposed—whether from an abhorrence of coercion or doubts about the universalizability of values—is philosophically distinct from the doctrine that there is no morality, although there is little question that adherents of the latter will strenuously argue the former as well.

If Will sees liberty in general more as the antithesis of sustained virtue than as the crucible out of which virtue is formed, his attitude towards capitalism is even less satisfying. It is not animus, by any means, but rather what George Gilder aptly labeled "the dirge of triumph."[3]

The 1980 Republican platform, Will argues for example,

is woven from two incompatible strands. "One is cultural conservatism. The other is capitalist dynamism. The latter dissolves the former." This, remarks Will in an aside, is perhaps the only point Marx got right. Capitalism, he continues, is a "relentless engine of change, a revolutionary inflamer of appetites, enlarger of expectations, and diminisher of patience." "Republicans," he warns, "see no connection between the cultural phenomena they deplore and the capitalist culture they promise to intensify." For Will, this tension between the bourgeois ethic and conserving social values presents an "especially vexing" dilemma—that of "deciding what is to be conserved, and how."

True conservatives can, however, and for the most part do, accept both the heritage of cultural conservatism and most of the reasoning of the defenders of *laissez-faire*. Rather than working against each other, freedom and tradition reinforce each other as both Hayek and Meyer convincingly argue in their respective works, *The Constitution of Liberty*[4] and *In Defense of Freedom*.[5] The tension Will sees between social conservatism and economic freedom is largely given the lie by history. The first century of America's nationhood, after all, saw both piety and morality, on the one hand, and freedom and the private property order, on the other. Will writes that "[c]apitalism means the liberation and incessant inflaming of appetites" the "predictable consequence" of which is "social disintegration." But that, as Will should know, is just not the way things happened. Social disintegration was brought on by slavery, not liberty, and, later, by economic intervention, not economic freedom.

Perhaps the matter will best be clarified if we consider the widely divergent defenses of capitalism of George Gilder and Ayn Rand. The one founds capitalism on altruism, the other on egoism. Yet neither is decidedly in the right, for capitalism is founded only on freedom. Philosophers, being philosophers, will impose on capitalism such attitudes, virtues, vices, and character as they believe free men and women will reflect. Thus, Gilder views man as altruistically motivated (of sorts), and a society of free men as altruistic, hence his almost poetic view of capitalism. Ayn Rand, in contrast, read human nature as deeply egoistic, and a society of free men as egoistic, hence her view of capitalism. The truth about man, of course, is somewhere in between, neither unremittingly egoistic, nor entirely selfless, and so it is with capitalist society.

Thus, when George Will writes that "[c]apitalism means the liberation and incessant inflaming of appetites," he is making less a proposition of economics, than a broad philosophical claim about the nature of man: This gives the claim added dignity, but less certainty. It is up to the reader to decide, ultimately, whether or not he shares Will's suspicion that when left free men attend "relentlessly" to their appetites.

---

1. This is primarily due to his seminal work, *Statecraft as Soulcraft* (Simon and Schuster, 1983).

2. George Will, *The Pursuit of Virtue and Other Tory Notions* (Simon and Schuster, 1982). All unattributed quotes in this chapter are from this volume.

3. George Gilder, *Wealth and Poverty* (Basic Books, 1981), p. 3.

4. F. A. Hayek, *The Constitution of Liberty* (Gateway Editions, 1972).

5. Frank Meyer, *In Defense of Freedom* (Henry Regnery Company, 1962).

8

Federalism: Bringing Economic Discipline into Politics

The nation continuously redistributes itself, as the voluntary choices of millions of individuals, families, and concerns make themselves felt. The North has gone South, the center of population has crossed the Mississippi, and those urban denizens with the will and means have fled the inner cities. Many view this process of adjustment with some anxiety, for the re-alignment of the national belts, as we have come to call them, may weaken a region's self-image and transform the character of the nation as a whole. The anxiety deepens into worry as one beholds the dissolution of neighborhoods in urban areas, for this is an ugly thing, an ugliness many are left behind to confront as it steadily worsens.

Yet, I hold a radically different view. To me the process is natural and beautiful: it is the American ideal at work: it is America at her best. Yes, it has its ugliness, but when one considers the cause, the effect, and the alternative, the beauty of such natural adjustment is plain.

The beauty of which we speak so passionately inheres in the conceit of a federation of sovereign states, for federalism is a noble system. Based on the humanizing conception of pluralism and the natural tendency of men to seek kindred kith and like minds, the federalist system enables the smaller statewide majorities to overrule the national majority locally in matters of local concern, thus allowing the people a greater measure of control over their own lives. It is not truly the states which have rights, but the citizenry by and with whose

---

Written after Ronald Reagan's resounding electoral triumph in 1980.

authority they are endowed. Among these rights is the right to self-determination, realized in full measure only by a highly federated system.

Such a system serves the interest of peace, as well. A large part of the reason our nation has weathered over two centuries of history is that, with the painful exception that nearly destroyed it, the American systems, political and economic, have not insisted on an artificial and imposed uniformity, the rigidity that is ripping apart our neighbor to the North[1] and perturbing finally even our archenemy to the East.

Today's centralism, in contrast, has relegated the states to the status of administrative serfs constantly faced with the choice "prostitute or destitute." These once-sovereign entities are finally learning that the inevitable result of dependence is subservience, a lesson the people, too, should learn. Untold waste of sinful proportions is another unavoidable result of large groups managing little persons and the small details of their lives. This, too, we have seen.

But worst of all, the quiet and automatic protection that federalism affords freedom has been weakened. For when the power to tax—that wellspring of tyranny which sparked the Revolutionary War—and the government encroachments thus enabled are concentrated at the state level, any substantial decrease in liberty results in the natural removal of the productive base to other states. The states are thus in competition for their means, with relative freedom one of their main dimensions of competition. This is true of nations, too, as witness the brain drain, the mass exodus of intellectuals, professionals, and producers from the Continent since the Second World War. Was America not formed by a like group of men, seeking refuge from the harsh doctrines of an authoritarian world and a new life amidst plenty? Has this country not been settled from sea to shining sea by men of distant lands seeking their fortunes in a free world?

This, then, is the cause of the population shifts we have

witnessed, this the answer to the query "Why have they gone?" The deterioration and decay of our once-majestic metropolises are, to use O'Casey's words, merely "outward and visible signs of an inward and spiritual disgrace."[2] It is the disgrace of governments which increasingly do more and more of what they should not do and less and less of what they should do. Urban flight is the natural reaction to the drive towards a more coercive society marked by the paradoxically simultaneous loss of both liberty and security. It is a philosophical, if implicit, judgment by the good people of this land on governments which presume to dictate to them above their level of tolerance and which no longer protect life, liberty, and property.[3]

What the social planners in the institutes for public policy see as the problem, the founding fathers saw as the solution. Erosion of the tax base is not the problem, high taxes are. Loss of children to bus is not the problem, busing is. Loss of subjects over whom to rule is not the problem, subjection is. The effect of free movement between semi-autonomous entities is to naturally correct localities which do not preserve liberty and maintain security; even so authoritarian a state as New York has been forced to take notice. The frightening alternative to this quiet and automatic protection, realized only partially under today's centralism, is an artificial and imposed uniformity which leaves no escape.

Freedom of association includes both the freedom to associate and the freedom not to associate. The flight of productive citizens from the tired cities, in particular, and the Northeast, in general, is a powerful use of both freedoms, a primal expression of the American ideal.

'Tis a cause for reflection that in 120 years the defenders of and detractors from the dignity of man have switched positions but the centers of power have not. Massachusetts, the birthplace of our Revolution and once the home of abolitionist ferment, is today the center of authoritarian scholarship and home to the establishment politicos who write such notions into law. Mississippi, once a slave state who gave her denizen and citizen to the Presidency of the Confederate States of America, today alone does not lay claim to the child's mind by compelling attendance at a government school unless his parents pay a private academy. She joins the Carolinas, a study shows, in hampering productive enterprises and citizens least. Once it was in New York that our federal constitution was so ably defended to the citizenry; today one must look to the state courthouses of Louisiana for a meet explication. Yet the ideas of the Northeast still hold sway, for liberalism is there defined and therefrom exported.

Now the winds of welcome change have swept across America, for in Ronald Reagan the statewide majorities throughout this land have chosen one of those Americans, few and far between, who deeply appreciate federalism for what it is and not for some one issue or the purposes of empty rhetoric. If this noble conception could once more be endeared to the American heart, what a boon it would be for the liberty-loving and what a blow to the apologists of a central, omnipotent authority. I can think of no better defense of such sentiment than the words of Jefferson:

> These principles form the bright constellation which has gone before us and guided our steps through an age of revolution and reformation. The wisdom of our sages and blood of our heroes have been devoted to their attainment. They should be the creed of our political faith, the text of civil instruction, the touchstone by which to try the services of those we trust; and should we wander from them in moments of error or of alarm, let us hasten to retrace our steps and to regain the road which alone leads to peace, liberty, and safety.[4]

The residential elections of the last decade, like the presidential election, are a repudiation of those who would replace the Constitution's Old Deal of liberty and prosperity with government, more government, and yet more government—while marauders roam our streets in search of criminal mischief and the ruthless abductors of whole continents move to engulf the world like a hungry, pathogenic amoeboid. The time has not come for the nation conceived in liberty to die. If we have faltered, it is for want of attention to the caveat of the Virginia Bill of Rights: "[N]o free government, or the blessings of liberty, can be preserved to any people, but . . . by frequent recurrence to fundamental principles."[5] So, "let us hasten to retrace our steps and to regain the road which alone leads to peace, liberty, and safety."

---

1. See Hans Sennholz, "Conflict in Canada," *The Freeman 31 (November 1981): 671–680.*

2. Sean O'Casey, *Inishfallen, Fare Thee Well* (Macmillan, 1949), p. 58.

3. As Herbert Hoover wrote, "[W]hether people know them by name or not, the principles of liberty and security are embedded in their daily thought and action." *The Challenge to Liberty* (Charles Scribner's Sons, 1934), p. 196.

4. Thomas Jefferson, *The Jeffersonian Cyclopedia* (John Foley, editor; Funk and Wagnalls Company, 1900), p. 981.

5. The Virginia Bill of Rights, *Sources of Our Liberties* (Richard Perry, editor; American Bar Foundation, 1959), p. 312.

9

Declarative Law

"[Legislators'] true office is to declare and enforce only our natural rights and duties and to take none of them from us . . ."

—Thomas Jefferson[1]

The law is imperative; it commands. Criminal law is a series of "Thou shalt not's." Regulatory law, a relatively new area of statutory endeavor (with, however, ancient roots), is a series of both "Thou shalt not's" and "Thou shalt's." Regulatory law of this sort often infringes on the natural rights of the parties, often presumes guilt in those regulated and requires them to prove themselves innocent, and often has perverse results, even results opposite from those intended. In short, and as people of all political persuasions are coming to realize, regulation is not the answer.

In this essay, I wish to develop an alternative to the imperative law which proscribes and prescribes. The alternative I am considering might be termed "declarative law," law which *describes*. Such a law would not conflict with libertarian values. It would not mandate prior restraint nor would it presume guilt. Most likely, the practical results of such law would be far superior to those of imperative law.

Basic civil law, both the common law and the statutory law, has the primary function of describing the responsibilities that one man has towards another. This function of the law comes from the basic Western tradition that the two senses of the word "responsible" are indissolubly linked; that is, if a man is responsible for an act in that he performed it, he is responsible for that act in that he is liable for its consequences.[2] This relation between the two senses of the word "responsible" can also be seen in Western religion which maintains a clear connection between virtue and reward, vice and punishment. And it can be seen in the market system where success is related to sensitivity to the economic needs of others and failure is related to insensitivity to the economic needs of others.

One of the ways, perhaps the principal way, in which civil law describes our respective responsibilities towards family members, friends, and business associates is through the law of negligence. Negligence is defined as "the failure to exercise that degree of care which, under the circumstances, the law requires for the protection of those interests of other persons which may be injuriously affected by the want of such care."[3] In other words, negligence is the "failure to exercise the care that a prudent person usually exercises."[4] Indeed in the law we are most often compelled to consider what "the ordinary, prudent man of average intelligence" would do and to use this fictitious man as the basis for deciding whether the answering party to a dispute has met his responsibilities.

New Jersey, which finds hosts who serve alcohol liable for the consequences of their guests' driving while intoxicated, has experimented with the idea of declarative law. Unfortunately, however, the two senses of "responsibility" are *not* linked here, since it is not the driver who is held responsible for the actions for which he is certainly, in the other sense of the word, responsible.

I should like to give two examples where existing imperative law might well be replaced by declarative law. The first is the New York State law requiring seat-belt use for all front-seat passengers under penalty of a fifty-dollar fine. Instead of a directive ordering drivers to take this precaution, a simple statement that they are liable at law to a civil suit in negligence and to criminal charges for manslaughter should suffice. In making such a declaration, the legislature would be doing no more than defining "prudence" and "ordinary care" in the light of the many studies showing the life-saving benefits of seat-belt use. And, also, some of the negatives that are associated with the laws mandating seat-belt use[5]—imperative law—would very likely be kept in check. It is within the scope of the legislative mandate to describe interpersonal responsibilities and to redefine these terms as needed. Naturally, there is no room in the freedom philosophy for legislation—imperative or declarative—requiring seat-belt use by the driver himself. The law exists to protect man from the folly of his fellow man, not from his own folly.

The second example is the New York City ordinance requiring landlords to install smoke detectors in all apartments at a maximum charge to tenants of ten dollars. Instead of this directive, we would prefer a declaration that given this new, inexpensive technology, its absence in the case of fire is negligent and exposes the landlord not only to civil liability but also to charges of manslaughter.

Now, there may be some apartment buildings in the poorer sections of town where tenants must choose between food now or protection from fire in the future. In that case, nothing prevents the tenants and the landlord from negotiating a waiver of responsibility—much like the liability-limiting waivers that are routinely signed prior to medical operations.

The advocate of regulation, hearing what we have proposed, will no doubt object that there is no prior restraint, that the remedies discussed—civil and criminal—exist only after the fact when it is too late. The answer, of course, to this objection is that while the state imposes no prior restraint, the market certainly does, on which immediate elaboration.

In a society based on declarative law, the need for liability insurance would be high and the insurance industry would surely develop schemes to protect their interests. Inspections by private insurance companies with millions of dollars at stake and whose inspectors may well have their jobs on the line will surely be more thorough than those done by disinterested bureaucrats working for indifferent agencies. Likewise, the expensive and cumbersome legal process of proving negligence when an insured company causes injury is now gladly undertaken by the insurance company. Furthermore, premiums for such insurance will be determined on the basis of the insured company's record and inspections. Companies with substantially higher premiums to pay than their competitors, and that includes companies insured on the basis of statistics without inspections, will soon find their prices noncompetitive and their customer-base shrinking. Likewise, a company without insurance at all is likely to be boycotted by most consumers: The existence of insured firms and consumers seeking security guarantees this. After all, companies which are insured have every incentive to capitalize on this fact by advertising.

It must be admitted, however, that on the free market, consumers who wish to bear the risk of dealing with uninsured companies—and in New York City consumers do this every time they choose a "gypsy" cab over a regulated, heavily insured "yellow" cab—either to save money or for convenience are free to do so. The claim we make is that the market adequately prevents and that the law adequately retaliates for harm done us by others, not that they prevent us from harming ourselves.

Besides liability insurance, insurance against extraordinary losses in business due to imprudence and any number of other insurance schemes might be contracted into. Neither I nor anyone else can know just how the insurance market would deal with product safety, economic security, employment hazards, and the like. But one can rest assured that under a regime of declarative law, the *ex post* penalties of the market and the law would be transmuted into preventive measures by all manner of individual and group schemes. If one could know just how the marketplace would work, the imperative for freedom would be a (merely) moral concern. Since one cannot predict the actions and decisions and interplay of millions of freely acting individuals—even with sophisticated mathematical models and computer simulations—the imperative for freedom is a practical concern as well.

---

1. Thomas Jefferson, *The Jeffersonian Cyclopedia* (John Foley, editor; Funk and Wagnalls Company, 1900), p. 492.

2. *American College Dictionary* (Random House, 1970), p. 1034, definitions 3 and 1.

3. *American College Dictionary* (Random House, 1970), p. 813.

4. *Webster's New Collegiate Dictionary* (G. & C. Merriam Company, 1974), p. 769.

5. John Semmens, "Do Seat Belt Laws Work?" *The Freeman 42 (July 1992): 280–281.*

10

Market Competition: Sensitivity to Others

Competition on the free and open market has long suffered criticism for its alleged imperfections. True market competition, it is averred, requires both buyers and sellers to have perfect knowledge of all alternatives. It likewise requires that buyers have full knowledge of the composition, use, and possible weaknesses of the product being offered for sale. It requires further that convenience of purchase—location, wrapping, queues, delivery, and the like—be equalized, and that extraneous factors such as personal relationships between buyer and seller be discounted.

Obviously, the argument continues, these conditions are never met in practice. Advertising, salesmanship, packaging, and displays take the place of perfect knowledge of the market. Product information is all too scarce, unless required by law. Convenience of purchase and other factors unrelated to the product itself bias market decisions in countless ways. Who has not often heard arguments along these lines,[1] together with suggestions for "correcting" the market and "compensating" for its imperfections?

But the critics betray that they do not grasp the subtlety of competition on the market, its many aspects and dimensions. The rigid price-quality contest portrayed with the aid of computer models is more nearly a caricature than an idealization of the multidimensional workings of the market, for as we shall see, market processes are broad enough to encompass the many facets of exchange mentioned above.

Once stated, the nature of competition on the market can hardly be denied: *Whatever* inclines a man to choose one product over another or to patronize one supplier over another is a dimension of competition. The man who seeks to influence the choices of his fellow man must thus be sensitive to *all* that may affect those choices. He must demonstrate an imaginative understanding of his neighbors' wants and then be ready, willing, and able to act on that understanding. Far from being a system of insensitivity as is so often charged, the market system uniquely rewards sensitivity to others in its broadest sense. Such sensitivity is marked along each of the many dimensions of competition and measured, in the aggregate, in profits or losses.

One such dimension, and the first hurdle facing a competitor, is the *quest for attention* from prospective buyers or sellers. As infants, we are unable to assimilate the stimulation which explodes all around us, and we tend only to that which is necessary, physically filtering out almost all the din of life. Later, as we mature, we learn to do the same on a more conscious level. It is doubtful whether we could long endure life without such filtering processes. Knowledge of all possibilities of exchange and all market opportunities is thus not only impossible; it is undesirable. What is both helpful and possible is knowledge of many of those opportunities that, given the chance, we would act upon.

Since those presenting possibilities for exchange or other market opportunities seek partners to their transactions, it is hardly surprising that market institutions for the dissemination of information about market opportunities have evolved so as to satisfy the demand for such matches.

Advertising, salesmanship, packaging, and displays are among these market institutions. They serve to penetrate the barriers of inattention we have erected to screen out much from our experience and surroundings that we do not deliberately seek. Indeed, successful market penetration is both unusual, statistically speaking, and mutually beneficial when it does occur. It is also quite an individual matter. It is the individual's special tastes, interests, and inclinations which will determine which appeals for attention will be successful and which will not.

That this is so is evidenced by the large investments in market research: Potential buyers are sampled to find out what publications they read, what media they attend to, what shops they frequent, what other interests or characteristics correlate to purchase of a given product, and so on. All this aids the competitor's understanding of why and when people choose his product. This is crucial, for as with all dimensions of competition, success in the quest for attention depends on understanding what makes others choose and acting upon that understanding.

But this is only the first hurdle, the first step of the marketing process. We may know the jingle and avoid the product, compliment the manager on his fine display but turn away empty-handed. Having secured the attention of consumers, the competitor must now demonstrate the value of his product to them at several levels.

At the first level, *persuasive marketing* will show that the need which the product satisfies is itself valuable to consumers. This is important since we have many competing needs to which we assign different subjective values. Advertisements extolling education are at this level. At the second level, persuasive marketing will show that the product being offered to the public best satisfies (or best satisfies at a given price) some underlying need of consumers. Advertisements by farmers' associations praising the virtues of good, wholesome milk as well as promotions of schooling are at this level. Then, at a third level, the producer must demonstrate the attractiveness of his particular brand.

This classification of the levels of marketing activity brings into relief the corresponding levels of competition: among needs, among products, and among producers. (A fourth level of competition, among suppliers offering the same stock, will be treated later.)

Yet to some extent this division, like any other, remains arbitrary, with its boundaries somewhat vague. Thus, advertising for many products (e.g., mouthwash, breakfast cereal, and book clubs) typically crosses levels, while for other products (e.g., food and shelter) the first level may not even be at issue. For still other products, those on which the producer holds a patent or copyright, the third level is not at issue.

It is well to remember that classifying competitive activity by level and dimension is much like classifying any part of free human action: it may be useful as an expository device, but it is not to be a means to argue for differential legal treatment based on the chosen categories.

Thus far, our discussion of the persuasive component of marketing, unlike our earlier treatment of the quest for attention, has been unidirectional: Sellers attempt to persuade buyers to exchange their money in exchange for the wares offered for sale. This is no accident, for while buyers, too, must often partake of the quest for attention, the remainder of the marketing process is nearly superfluous when the most marketable commodity, money, is offered in exchange. The first level of marketing activity is obviated by its very nature as a medium of exchange: Its need lies in the need for any economic good whatsoever. In theory, the second and third levels of competition apply to money as much as to anything else. The contest between gold and silver typifies the former, while that between institutions offering warehouse receipts or promissory notes redeemable in specie typifies the latter. In practice, however, since the state has usurped the market in money, there is no real competition along the dimension of persuasive marketing among buyers.

That success in marketing is determined by the degree to which the competitor and his publicist understand the needs and wants of consumers, as consumers see them, does not mean that marketing of a product cannot seek to ***change*** the way people choose to allocate their resources, satisfy their needs, or decide among competing needs. On the contrary, that is its *raison d'être*. It does mean, however, that effective marketing is based on understanding how people currently make their choices, including how, why, and under what conditions they might be influenced—they might choose—to alter their patterns of choice.

Another dimension of competition often ignored in models of "perfect" competition is *information*. Information, it should be recalled, is an economic good: It is both scarce and valued.[2] Information about a product will thus sometimes be available and sometimes not, depending on whether it is more profitable to procure and disseminate it or more profitable not to do so. This, in turn, depends on whether consumers value the information more than the resulting increment in price or not.

Thus, food companies providing the extensive testing necessary to label cholesterol content to the nearest milligram only under threat of harassment by government agents are not denying consumers information they "ought" to have. Such information, like any economic good, is provided in quantities determined by the intersection of its demand curve with its supply curve. If rather little information is provided, this indicates not malevolent exploitation of ignorance, but rather that consumers are unwilling to pay the price that would generate a greater stock. That is a decision that should be left to them. Under the market system it is.

When the demand for accurate information about a product is sufficiently high so as to support the price needed to call forth the supply, competition will assure its presence. But, the critics contend, doesn't such simple-minded supply-demand analysis suppose that the information in question is *neutral*? What if provision of the information would cause the demand curve to fall off sharply? What recourse do buyers have when the product fails to perform adequately? And what prevents the unscrupulous seller from masking defects or other information which reflects undesirably on his product? If the market is based on the profit motive and incentives, what about cases where the incentives are apparently in all the wrong places: to be insensitive rather than sensitive, to be unscrupulous rather than honorable, and so on? There is genuine moral concern underlying these questions, concerns that we now address.

As usual, critics of the market believe that if government does not regulate, there will be chaos. In reality, however, liberty is self-regulating and the free market turns chaos into order. Specifically, the consumer has several sources of protection from the competitor who shields nonneutral information: the law, other competitors, other consumers, and himself.

By recourse to the law, we do not refer to regulatory law, "consumer law," or any of the other new areas of statutory endeavor—all of which, in greater or lesser degree, presume guilt in the producer—but rather to the common law, as it has developed over the centuries. If outright fraud is perpetrated or the warranty of merchantability is breached, the purchase lacks informed consent and redress by the courts is in order. Likewise, the time has long passed when poison could be sold as medicine—violence done to person or property, willfully or through negligence, is not specially protected by its perpetration through economic transactions. But recourse to the law, as the critics remind us, is a cumbersome and expensive process and one which is necessarily undertaken only after the improper action is taken and the damage is suffered. If the law is not to presume guilt, it can sanction retaliatory measures only. Preventive measures must be left to the marketplace, a topic to which we now turn.

Circumscribing the actions of competitors on the market are other competitors who seek business, consumers who seek the best buy, and groups of these acting in concert to protect their common interests. To begin with, it must be understood that just as there can never be complete product information, there can never be neutral product information. All information about a product affects the choices of the consumer and is thus nonneutral. Even information about proper use or care for the product may change a consumer's mind about its purchase. And if it is absent, it may present a risk to consumers buying the product or impose the cost of obtaining the information elsewhere. Risk, it might be added, is central here. The less complete the information, the greater the risk. The willingness to bear that risk is ultimately up to the consumer and it is he, therefore, who has ultimate responsibility for his purchases.

But everyone prefers to operate under a minimum of risk and a maximum of information. Thus information becomes a dimension of competition. Sure, producers might prefer to offer their wares without the information that is a necessary concomitant; but the existence of other competitors who provide more information and consumers who value such information leaves them no such choice. Other competitors may even supply the decidedly nonneutral information that the wayward producer shields from view. News organizations, responding to the same demand, may also expose it. Even if not revealed, however, the absence of information, like the presence of discouraging information, is often enough to deter the consumer from making the purchase.[3]

There will be instances where information cannot be verified by consumers even when present and where substantial danger would result from poor quality and an accompanying lack of information, as with medication. In such cases, the after-the-fact penalties exacted by the law—in damages, including possible punitive damages—and the market—in loss of future sales—would be correspondingly high. Too high to risk. There can be little doubt that such companies would take out insurance. They have every incentive to do so, *especially* if they are not conscientious. But the insurance companies have every incentive to see to it that claims are not made and, if made, not collected. They will thus act to guard their assets. Inspections by private insurance companies with their revenue at stake and with inspectors whose jobs may be on the line will surely be more thorough than those of disinterested government agents employed by the state. Moreover, the expensive and cumbersome legal process of proving fraud or negligence when an insured company does market a dangerous product is now gladly undertaken by the insurance company.

Premiums for such insurance will be determined on the basis of the company's record and inspections. A company with substantially higher premiums than its competitors, and that includes companies insured on the basis of statistics without inspections, will soon find its prices noncompetitive and its customer-base eroding rapidly. A company without insurance at all is likely to be boycotted by most consumers. The existence of other, insured firms and consumers seeking security guarantees this. Once again, producers and suppliers who are insured have every incentive to advertise the fact, and to attach inspection labels with the name of the certifying company onto their wares. (The insurance company may either insure the client company against liability or extraordinary loss of business due to product damage, or insure the consumers directly. The certifying company need not even be known as an insurance company—it could be a magazine—but in this respect it will function as one.)

It must be admitted, however, that on the free market consumers who wish to bear the risk of buying from an uninsured, uninspected drug company either to save money or for other reasons are free to do so. The market adequately prevents harm done to us by others; it does not prevent us from harming ourselves.

Notice, though, what has happened. Through the complex interplay of a series of market incentives, retaliatory legal and market penalties have been transmuted into preventive measures. Such insurance schemes as we have described are not more widespread only because government heavily regulates both the insurance industry and the potential client industries. Because government has effectively monopolized and usurped the insurance business, some of the industry's most natural constituencies have never been fully cultivated.

Another market mechanism for protecting the consumer which has been adopted under pressure of competition is the guarantee. Because prior information about the quality of some goods and services is difficult to obtain (e.g., repair services), guarantees have become a standard substitute. Although this remedy works only after the transaction, it both removes the incentive for and imposes a cost on making a sale under false pretenses. Thus, once again, a subsequent remedy is transmuted by market incentives into a preventive measure.

If one wishes evidence that competition promotes rather than stifles the dissemination of product information, one need only compare the readily available information about goods and services offered on the market with that available about services offered by the government. It is legend that taxpayers inquiring about government services are shifted endlessly from office to office in a vain quest. Despite reams of published material detailing every last function of government, taxpayers are often unable to obtain answers to even the simplest of questions. Likewise, it is interesting to note that just those areas of enterprise devoid of competition, notably utility and other companies with direct or indirect grants of monopoly power by the state, are the least satisfying when it comes to information about their products and prices. Computing the price for even a relatively simple service often entails poring through pages of cross-referenced tables with notes and addenda. Some of this excess is due to the absence of competition decreed by the state. Not surprisingly, much of it is the result of the company's response to the state agencies which take it upon themselves to set a "just price," a task which belongs to the market.

Yet another market mechanism that competitors must worry about is the voluntary inspections and standards of trade groups and consumer "watchdog" associations. Yes, companies can deny these entry and data, but to many consumers that would be *prima facie* evidence of failure to meet those standards. Yes, the standards themselves may be weak or poorly enforced, but if demand for the product or underlying need is even reasonably elastic (as it almost always is), the incentives are in all the right places: Weak or poorly enforced standards cause the public to view the entire industry with distrust (this has happened with the mass media, for example) and that is bad for business. Furthermore, consumer groups which undertake such projects as comparative rating of products, product testing, determining best buys, and listing appliances together with their specifications can be a formidable opponent of shoddy production practices. Nevertheless, as we remarked about insurance, neither trade groups nor consumer associations have developed on the market to the extent that manifest concern—consumer demand—would call forth. These initiatives, too, have largely been usurped by the activities of government regulators.

It must be admitted, however, that at times none of these sources of consumer protection will operate. The presence of residual fraud, misrepresentation, or omission of damaging information that obtains under the market system is often defended by the advocates of capitalism as the price of freedom from prior controls, constant supervision, and other collectivist measures. This defense was most eloquently articulated by Herbert Hoover in *The Challenge to Liberty,* written at the start of the New Deal:

> There is no doubt that the weeds of economic abuse will grow in the garden of Liberty. The fertile soil of this garden also produces the fine blossoms of enterprise and invention. Evil as the weeds are, it is far

> better to expend the labor to extirpate them than to lose the whole garden through the blight of tyranny.[4]

The simple truth, however, is that *no* system can eliminate abuse. The market system at least minimizes it. Abuse is the price of being human, not the price of being free. The quality and safety of products manufactured under command economies, where every stage of the production process is under supervision and subject to government standards and controls, is a powerful indication of this.

When the market fails, planning must fail spectacularly, for the mistakes of central planners, unlike those of entrepreneurs, are centrally imposed on the entire economy. Where the market and the law under which it operates may at least take action after an abuse occurs—and, very often, before, as we discussed above—the system of planning with its unnatural disjunctions between profits and success, losses and failure, and responsibility for actions and liability for their consequences remains indifferent. The market attends to economic signals which duly report mistakes. Planners, on the other hand, having destroyed or distorted economic calculation, attend only to political signals which report whatever meets the party line.

Before concluding this discussion of product information, we should take note of the moral issue involved in forcing the release of information. In finding the forced recitation of the Pledge of Allegiance by public school children unconstitutional, the Supreme Court declared the right not to speak at least as protected as the right to speak.[5] Circumscriptions of speech generally involve a mild contraction of choice, whereas coerced speech eliminates all choice. It is thus a mark of how far the artificial dichotomy between economic and personal freedom has permeated our law that, despite the reasoning above, producers and suppliers are daily forced to make all manner of declarations, issue all sorts of lists, and post a wide variety of information. The forced release of information is not only inefficient and counterproductive; it is also a violation of privacy and the natural right of free expression. Notice that here, as with so much else, what is moral and what is pragmatic are harmoniously aligned.

In addition to information about the product, information on pricing is also an aspect of competition. For example, computer-printed and -itemized bills, electronic scales, comprehensive price labeling, and machine built-in pricing each lessens the risk of overcharging consumers and their apprehension of being overcharged. Consumers may thus be inclined to prefer the supplier who provides this information over one who does not. As always, the amount of information provided is determined by the supply and demand schedules.

The information dimension is one along which buyers, too, must compete. When the seller accepts personal checks or purchases on the books, he exchanges his merchandise for something about the value of which his information is incomplete. In doing so, he bears a risk in return for a hoped-for profit from the policy (which includes gains from cash transactions by customers attracted by the policy) after subtracting defaults, penalties, and lost interest. Buyers who provide more information (using, say, a major credit card, subject to on-line verification) are at an advantage in dealing with sellers who value that resource highly. Other buyers, transacting with sellers less concerned with this, gain from paying in a more convenient fashion or at a later date.

For all this, however, price and quality do remain the most important dimensions of competition, for they epitomize the process of exchange: value given for value. Yet price and quality, even aside from the various marketing and information dimensions, do not entirely exhibit the full richness of competition.

Convenience of purchase is a most important dimension of competition in an age of harried consumers, and *pleasantness of purchase* has been important in every age. Such factors as the location of the store, the lengths of its queues, the quality of its wrapping of products, the availability of delivery, the interior decorations, displays, music, the courtesy and helpfulness of sales personnel, and the like must all be taken into account by the competitor who would know success, since consumers allow them to affect their choices.

True, inconvenience of purchase could be figured in as *part* of the price and pleasantness of purchase as *part* of what is received, necessitating no change in the traditional price-quality model. The problem with such an approach, however tenable in the abstract, is that the monetary value that consumers place on such aspects of exchange as information, convenience of purchase, and pleasantness of purchase varies with the time of day, the consumers' moods, how tired they are, and a myriad other factors. The real world, that is, is in a constant state of flux, with the array of subjective values consumers hold being adjusted constantly. This reflects neither whimsicality nor irrationality on the part of the consumers, but rather rational and adaptive adjustment to external and internal changes.

These often elusive factors—hard to identify, harder to quantify, still harder to track as they change—may defy mathematical models and computer simulations of competition. But in an age of relative affluence, with small differences in price of lesser import, these factors become increasingly valued by consumers as the reader's own experiences measured against that of his grandparents will attest. Far from being extraneous factors that "bias" market decisions, convenience and pleasantness of purchase are integral parts of the exchanges of value for value that collectively comprise what is figuratively known as the marketplace.

A final aspect of competition which deserves special mention is *location*. Location is a part of virtually every dimension of competition one can imagine: the quest for attention, persuasive marketing, information, convenience of purchase, pleasantness of purchase. Location also figures at many levels: which country, which province, which town, which district. At the higher levels, prevailing wage rates and business climate as determined by the presence or absence of particular government interventions are often the most important factors. At the lower levels, centrality of location, proximity of resources, accessibility by public transportation, proximity to or distance from competitors (depending on the business), and the like are often more important.

Location is also a factor within a shop, even within a product (think of a newspaper, magazine, or book!). Indeed, it would be quite impossible for the casual observer to list all the dimensions or levels at which location figures, but even a cursory examination of one's own patterns of economic choice—consumption—should persuade one of both its ubiquitousness and importance.

In sum, while competition occurs on many levels, along many dimensions, and with a richness as full as human choices can be, success is measured only in the aggregate, by profits or losses. The competitor will thus be told in no uncertain terms whether or not he is succeeding, and to what extent. The market will never tell him why. Just how he favorably or unfavorably affects the choices of those with whom he transacts is something to which he must be sensitive: That is the essence of competition on the market.

---

1. See, for example, Gerson Antell, "Imperfect Competition," *Economics: Institutions and Analysis* (Amsco, 1970), pp. 100–103.

2. See, for example, Gary North, "Exploitation and Knowledge," *The Freeman 32 (January 1982): 3–11.*

3. One example of this is ratings of charities according to market standards by the (private) National Charities Information Bureau and, separately, by the Philanthropic Advisory Service of the Council of Better Business Bureaus. In addition to compiling lists of charities that conform to generally accepted standards and those that don't conform, a list of the numerous organizations which refuse to disclose the data necessary for an informed evaluation is published. I, for

one, will never extend myself to such a charity: Funds are scarce and the number of charities that openly comply with standards are numerous. Why risk wasting precious funds?

4. Herbert Hoover, *The Challenge to Liberty* (Charles Scribner's Sons, 1934), pp. 166–167.

5. *West Virginia State Board of Education v. Barnette,* 319 U.S. 624.

II. THE FREE MARKET AND THE REDISTRIBUTIVE STATE IN ACTION

1

Are There Too Many Lawyers?

It might appear that the question, "Are there too many lawyers?" reeks of the discontent with the market that still prevails among the elites who support the discredited models of the managed economy. Indeed, given world events, no one should have to answer questions such as "Are there too many shoemakers?" It is simply up to consumers willing to pay certain amounts for shoes, accessories, and repair—the demand schedule—and up to would-be shoemakers willing to offer their services at certain wage rates—the supply schedule—to jointly determine the number of shoemakers.

Closer analysis, however, as well as some startling data suggest that lawyers providing legal services to plaintiffs are in a class of their own. Yes, there is a market for legal services and, yes, a free-market society does have a place for actions at law. Notwithstanding this, however, legal services are fundamentally different from other services, simply because lawyers must use the law—the State—to give plaintiffs the property of defendants. Today's plaintiffs' bar is expert at using the law to attain wealth by what Albert Jay Nock called "the political means" rather than "the economic means"—i.e., by the redistribution of existing wealth, rather than the creation of new wealth.[1] Indeed, it is clear that the very same ethos that informs legislative redistribution is responsible for judicial redistribution: the cultivation of a state of mind which asserts the victimhood of select groups. While legislative redistribution typically focuses on race, gender, ethnicity, poverty, and similar states of "victimhood," judicial redistribution typically fo-

---

Patrick J. Vincent, co-author.

cuses on class interests, among them: tenants, consumers, employees, and those suffering from injury, illness, or loss of function due to unfortunate accidents that are no one's fault.

Besides the moral point, judicial intervention—like all strictly redistributive processes—results in a far less robust economy, one designed to avoid judicial redistribution, rather than one designed to create and produce. Empirical support for this conclusion abounds: (1) The United States has only five percent of the world's population, but has fully seventy percent of the world's lawyers! (2) We spend more than eighty billion dollars a year on direct costs of litigation and on insurance premiums and a total of three hundred billion dollars on indirect efforts to avoid liability. (3) The threat of litigation has caused 47 percent of manufacturers to withdraw products from the market. (4) The threat of litigation has also discouraged no less than 25 percent of manufacturers from some types of product research. (5) Largely due to the fees brought in by the plaintiffs' bar, our trial lawyers are the best-paid attorneys in the world. (6) *Per capita,* we have thirty percent more lawsuits than do the Japanese, one of our main competitors in the creation of wealth. (7) In Japan, the ratio of engineers to lawyers is 20:1, but in this country it is $2\frac{1}{2}$:1![2]

At this point it is well to make some qualifications. First, it *is* true that the market may decide that the potential harm of a risky good or service outweighs its potential benefits. The market properly both embraces and limits risk, as reflected in the supply and demand schedules for risky goods and services. Second, liability for civil wrongs—torts—remains a powerful disincentive for fault, and one that works. Third, contingency fees *do* allow access to the courts by those with a genuine complaint who cannot afford to retain counsel.

Unfortunately, however, far too many folks welcome the chance to be plaintiffs, since being a plaintiff is cost-free. The contingency-fee cases that the plaintiffs' bar handles—principally malpractice and product liability cases—allow any number of lawsuits regardless of the merits of the complaints. Indeed, since there is no effective penalty for frivolous lawsuits, the demand schedule is potentially infinite, restrained only by a vague sense in ordinary citizens on what is properly the subject of a suit at law and what is not. But the statistics above show nothing if not that such sensibilities are rapidly disappearing, and when obstetricians stop delivering babies *en masse,* it is time to restore some limits on the demand schedule for lawyers.

The most obvious reform, long advocated by many, is to require unsuccessful plaintiffs to pay the defendants' legal fees. A second reform is to make the system inherently less redistributive, by changing the burden of proof. The present system allows redistribution from defendant to plaintiff when there is a "fair preponderance of the credible evidence," i.e., with just 51 percent of the merits in the matter. Whatever happened to the old adage, "Possession is nine-tenths of the law"? The standard currently used for some federal suits, "clear and convincing evidence," is much to be preferred.

It cannot be emphasized enough that the only way to genuinely improve the lot of the masses is by the creation of new wealth, rather than the redistribution of existing wealth. As Governor Richard Lamm put it, "No nation in history has ever sued its way to greatness."[3]

---

1. Albert Jay Nock, *Our Enemy, The State* (Hallberg Publishing Corporation, 1983), p. 46.

2. David Gergen, "America's Legal Mess," *U.S. News and World Report,* August 19, 1991, p. 72.

3. *Ibid.*

2

Why Are There So Many Social Issues?

One of today's major functions of the Supreme Court is to decide between competing claims based on the rights of the parties to the dispute. In balancing the parties' rights, at least one side and often both sides find their rights circumscribed.

As we shall show by means of several well-chosen examples, this function of the High Court (and, for that matter, lower courts and legislatures as well) would be rendered nugatory in a libertarian society. In each case, there is some underlying government intervention which forces the conflict between the liberties of the parties and makes a choice between them inevitable.

Consider, for example, the issue of prayer in the public schools. Proponents say, correctly, that the Founders of the Republic never meant to exclude God from the classroom, that prayer has never harmed a soul, and that it remains voluntary. Opponents argue, correctly, that students who are "different" and don't pray with the group will be singled out for unpopularity and that a child under such peer pressure has no volition to speak of. They add, correctly, that parents, not schools, should minister to the religious needs and beliefs of children.

And so the issue is left for the Supreme Court; it must rule on an unending stream of cases: moments of silence, student-led prayer groups, prayer after school hours but on school property, and the like. Whatever the Court decides, however, and no matter how carefully or idiosyncratically it draws the line between the religious liberty and educational freedom of the various constituencies, someone must surrender a piece of his freedom.

When I am asked whether I favor prayer in the public schools, however, the answer is quite a bit simpler. No lines to be drawn, no careful circumscriptions of rights, and no balancing of one man's liberty against that of another man. "I do not favor public schools," I reply, "and therefore do not reach your question." The key to the controversy is not "prayer" but "public." It is the underlying government intervention of compulsory schooling and tax-financed, government schools which force the competing claims to a head. Were the schools to be all private, there would be no problem, as each parent selected the school which best meets the interests of his or her child as the parent defines it.

As another example, consider the demonstrations led by neo-Nazis in Jewish areas. Opponents say, correctly, that hatred has no place in a society of refugees, diverse ethnic groups, and freedom. They add, correctly, that the Founders never intended such "speech" to be free, making, as they did, a careful distinction between freedom and license. Proponents say, correctly, that the test of free expression in a free society is only met when that which is spoken is repugnant to the great majority of people. They add, correctly, that truth is best served by an unbridled freedom of expression and that hatred is unlikely to truly grip America today.

Again, however, someone must surrender a piece of his liberty, no matter how the question is decided. Were streets to be private property, as libertarians have proposed, the owners would determine what may or may not take place on their property and the government would not be called on to choose between its citizens. With public ownership of the streets and byways of America, there is simply no way to accommodate the claims of both those who want a public forum and those who do not want their sensibilities lacerated by Nazi "speech."

Most controversies of the day can be reduced to an underlying government intervention, and since government interventions are ubiquitous, it is no surprise that not a day passes without there being a major news item on a social issue.

Let us elaborate. Similar to our first case, we have the furor over sex education and condom distribution, phonics *vs.* the look-say method of learning to read, values clarification, death education, evolution and Creation, and the like. Likewise, public religious displays, smoking in public, and soliciting of funds by beggars and certain religious denominations in public places are all similar to our second example. In each case, the controversy would disappear with privatization, and the rights of *all* parties would be respected.

3

Abortion: Is Pro-Choice a Libertarian Position?

Those who favor abortion on demand use the rhetoric of libertarianism to justify their position. Hence, there is much talk of compulsory pregnancy, forced childbirth, lack of control over one's own body (bodily parts), absence of reproductive choice, and so on. Faced with such language, pro-lifers often retreat into a discussion of liberty *vs.* license, liberty *vs.* order, or the primacy of the right to life over other rights. These arguments, while not without merit, yield far too much ground to the abortion advocates. For the simple truth is that freedom is not counterbalanced by a higher (or even simply other) good when abortion is proscribed. Liberty, recall, is the *absence* of coercion—while abortion, of course, is a coercive act. Hence, to outlaw abortion is merely to array societal forces against private coercion, a legitimate retaliatory use of force in the libertarian tradition. Indeed, it is rather a contradiction in terms to speak of "the liberty to rob, rape, or murder." Such actions are all very definitely coercive interventions in the lives of others and can hardly be justified as permitted by a doctrine of noninterference!

Writing in *Power and Market,* economist-philosopher Murray Rothbard points out the sufficiency of "Every man may act as he freely chooses" as a definition of liberty.[1] The proviso usually added—"provided he respects the like freedom of others"—is redundant given the universal quantifier "every." For, as Rothbard notes, if one man's freely chosen action is the assault or robbery of another man, then the victim is deprived of living or acting as *he* chooses and liberty does not obtain. This is just the situation with abortion: The control being sought is not over one's own body but over another's. That is not freedom, there being no coherent notion of freedom which includes the freedom to coerce.

This brings us to the question of choice. No movement is more on the side of reproductive choice and strict control over one's own body than the pro-life movement. After all, the essence of the pro-life position is respect for the reproductive choice made by the couple and flowing directly from the control the woman had over her own body. The abortion advocates, in contrast, do not respect the choice made and seek control over the body—indeed, the very life—of another.

Talk of compulsory pregnancy or forced childbirth is little more than an ideological distraction. To be sure, the pregnancy might have been an undesired consequence of the desired sexual intimacy. But that is compulsory or coercive only in the sense that a man who throws a baseball a great distance for the pleasure he receives can claim that the resulting damage done to a neighbor's window was "against his will" and that the untoward consequence was "imposed" on him. It used to be understood that the laws of nature were not subject to congressional repeal or voiding by the courts and that natural results flowing from voluntary actions are in no meaningful sense of the word "imposed."

The contrary of this simple enough proposition undercuts all of Western moral and legal theory, one reason of many why the abortion debate is not just a social issue. If our civilization is held together by any single notion, it is surely that the two senses of "responsibility" are inextricably intertwined: If a man is responsible for an action in that he *performed* it, he is responsible for it in that he is *liable* for the consequences. The religious belief that virtue is rewarded and sin punished is so premised. Our system of free enterprise is also rooted in this idea: Every man receives neither an equal return on his labor, nor one based on need, nor one deemed fair by social theorists or experts in so-called comparable worth, but rather one based on what has been done for others as *they* see it. Reward flows from fruitful efforts, profits from successes, and losses from failures. How could it be otherwise? Always, in the Western tradition, it has been tacitly accepted that responsibility in one sense flows from responsibility in the other sense. That is what makes social co-operation possible, the single principle which makes associations with our fellow human beings other than fraught with continuous and overwhelming uncertainty, risk, and danger.

Yet it is just this central, civilizing principle that is under attack by those who wrongly label themselves "pro-choice." The relation between the dual notions of responsibility leaves no doubt as to whether or not a parent is responsible, financially and otherwise, for the care and life of his child.

It is not choice the abortionists desire, but the revocation of choice and its natural consequences. They wish to roam the world acting as they will *and* to be "free" from the "oppressive" consequences of their own actions. To be responsible for everything, yet responsible for nothing. This we cannot allow. It is not liberty, not choice, but escape from both.

---

1. Murray Rothbard, *Power and Market* (Institute for Humane Studies, 1970), p. 179.

4

On *Feminism and Freedom*

Feminism and Freedom,[1] the subject of this essay review, is a scholarly book which treats of the implications of contemporary feminism for human freedom. Philosopher Michael Levin opens with an example (Berkman *v.* NYFD) which nicely illustrates his two theses: first, that men and women are different and that the differences are by no means attributable primarily to socialization (environmentalism); second, that refusal to recognize these differences on the part of the state will necessarily lead to "corrective" and coercive state action which deforms society and the individuals who compose it. As Levin writes, "Although feminism speaks the language of liberation, . . . options, and the removal of barriers, these phrases invariably mean their opposites and disguise an agenda at variance with the ideals of a free society." This outcome is inevitable, Levin argues. "Since innate gender differences express themselves as differences in the typical preferences of men and women . . . the equalization of the sexes in personal behavior and in the work world demands implacable surveillance and interference. In the end," he continues, "it is impossible to overcome the biological inevitability of sex roles, but it is possible to try—and to violate liberal values in the process."

In the succeeding chapter, Levin struggles to find a workable definition of feminism—one which feminists themselves can accept and one which provides a systematic framework for the understanding of the broad areas of social concern which somehow involve gender differences. He arrives at a suitable, four-point definition after surveying feminist writing from John Stuart Mill in 1869 to the present day. The razor-sharp analysis here is as well done a process of intellectual discovery as any. One point that bears mention is Levin's argument that since most stereotypical female behavior occurs voluntarily, it cannot be illiberal; on the contrary, measures taken to forcibly change this situation are illiberal. This is not recognized because, Levin writes, "The idea that voluntary sex-typed behavior is inauthentic explains the readiness to call for state action that is prominent in the feminist political agenda." "Inauthentic" because "while women . . . may be doing what they want, the conditions under which their wants were formed were constrained." But since "everyone's wants would have been somewhat different had he been raised differently," Levin continues, "then [by this logic] no one is free"—not just women with a traditional socialization. Indeed, many feminists treat (innate) preferences as obstacles to be overcome.

Levin then gives a convincing explanation of the curious fact that virtually all well-known feminists are socialists. He writes, "It is psychologically difficult to regard a situation as extremely unjust without wishing to deploy [force, here] the state against it," especially since the sweeping changes that many feminists espouse "cannot be achieved without state coercion."

The next two chapters of *Feminism and Freedom* make the case against pure environmentalism, which is a view that "implies that any significant statistical disparity in outcomes for men and women is due to outright discrimination or more subtly inequitable social forces"—rather than arising from innate preferences. These chapters are exceedingly well written and are copiously documented. Indeed, the second of these chapters is essentially a short, scientific survey on sex differences, amply supported by the scientific literature.

Following this, two chapters deal with the inequalities of opportunity imposed on individuals in order to eradicate inequalities of outcome and the intolerable—to feminists—conclusion that men and women are better at different tasks and are not fungibles. Everything from affirmative action to comparable worth is discussed here and in a civil and scholarly, if not dispassionate, tone.

The remaining chapters discuss the pervasiveness of feminist thinking and its frequent reliance on the state to translate this thinking into public policy in several different domains: education at all levels, sports, and language. Space considerations prevent a detailed review of the many fine points made about each of these domains, but even an initially unsympathetic reader is bound to come away with an entirely different outlook, as did the present writer.

Before closing, one of Levin's more powerful chapters, "Sex, the Family, and the Liberal Order," deserves mention. Levin quotes Benjamin Barber: "The slogans were extraordinary: marriage was hell, sex was political, coitus was killing, married women were prostitutes, babies were traps, intercourse was rape, love was slavery, families were prisons, and men were enemies." While as Levin admits, "Feminists have for the most part moderated their tone," the residue of this sort of radicalism remains. Thus Levin discusses sex, motherhood, the family, divorce, work outside the home, day care, abortion, and homosexuality from the perspective of feminists, from the perspective of the state, and from the perspective of someone who rejects most feminist doctrine.

The book as a whole is remarkable for its clarity of thought and vision, its civil tone, and its excellent documentation—both through numerous examples in the text and through footnotes.

---

1. Michael Levin, *Feminism and Freedom* (Transaction Books, 1987). All unattributed quotes in this chapter are from this volume.

5

Pay Television and Freeloading

A large number of American homes, recently estimated as over 100,000, are now equipped with special antennae, decoders, converters, and other electronic gadgetry capable of receiving the signals from pay television satellites or earthbound microwave transmitters.

Faced with such a large number of potential clients who prefer to freeload, the pay television industry is fighting back. Arguing that the unauthorized reception of their signals is a violation of their property rights, the industry convinced the FCC to issue an injunction prohibiting such reception. A federal circuit court of appeals upheld the order, thus stamping into law the common notion that these freeloaders are "pirates of the air" or "basement thieves."

Looking at the matter on its face, there is ample reason to be suspicious. First, federal courts have not shown overmuch concern for the property rights of corporations, preferring instead long and learned disquisitions on "the public good" and the exact meaning of a "taking." As for the regulatory agencies, they have been downright hostile to the very concept of private property (i.e., that ownership implies control). Second, there is no greater protection of personal liberty than the rights of private property.[1] An abridgment of liberty in the name of property rights is thus automatically suspect.

Examining the matter in more detail, it is clear that broadcast frequencies, commonly referred to as "airwaves," are real property. Like other real property, they are properly acquired by appropriation and continuous possession and use over a period of years, not by government distribution.

Now real property cannot be stolen, but it can be illegally

occupied. This is known as trespass, the prevention of which is properly a function of government, part of its mandate to secure our rights.

In considering how one illegally occupies a broadcast frequency, we must distinguish between transmission and reception. When one transmits on another's frequency, he is indeed a broadcast pirate for he illegally occupies that which is someone else's. It makes no difference that the offender may broadcast from his basement: Is the man who launches a missile into his neighbor's yard any less guilty because he owns the launch pad?

When one receives another's transmission in the privacy of his home, however, he neither damages nor occupies the broadcaster's real property and has not violated anyone's rights. If the broadcaster chooses to dump what economists call positive externalities, such as the entertainment emanating from his airwaves, on another's private property, the property owner is free to take advantage of this. One must distinguish between the airwaves, the real property that the broadcaster owns, and the programs, the positive externalities the freeloader enjoys, despite the fact that the latter originate from the former.

Philosopher Robert Nozick makes a similar point in his landmark *Anarchy, State and Utopia* in disputing the idea that someone's positive behavior towards me necessarily requires reciprocation or compensation, even when he acts voluntarily and without my contractual agreement to pay.[2] The core of this idea is that all freeloading is theft, an idea that can easily be adapted to justify all manner of anti-libertarian state endeavors. Nozick asks whether a man who throws books into my yard from his yard can demand payment. Here it is from his yard (real property he owns) that the books (analogous to positive externalities) enter my yard (real property I own).

Although it may be felt that airwaves and programs are somehow different from yards and books, in practice we are quite ready to grant the similarity. Is there anyone who would claim that a CB radio buff who demands payment after being entertaining for a bit is entitled to use the coercive apparatus of the state to exact it? Pay television companies differ from the CB user only in that they entertain professionally, at considerable expense, and for their livelihood. But if the greater extent of the freeloading is all that separates the two cases, then if one is not theft, neither is the other.

If anything, programs and airwaves present an even weaker case for mandatory compensation than the likes of books and yards. Consider the case of a man's apples falling into his neighbor's yard. Leaving aside the separate question of whether such placement (of the tree and/or apples) can be enjoined or whether rent (compensation for the negative externalities) can be exacted, the man is entitled to the return of his apples. He has lost personal property which can be restored to him. But programs dissipate as they are watched, and at the show's end, the broadcaster has whatever he had before. Put plainly, there is neither anything to return nor anything that was lost. Only when lost income is a result of some rights-violating activity is compensation in order: Lost income cannot be used as the basis of a claim for compensation.

At the heart of the confusion lie several mistaken analogies. First, there is the sentiment expressed by Assistant FCC Counsel Norman Blumenthal: "It's like sneaking into a movie theater." Not at all. It's rather like viewing a drive-in movie from your living room window or watching your neighbor's Fourth of July fireworks display from the comfort of your backyard hammock. In each case, you receive benefits without payment, but without fault, for to be a thief you must positively violate someone's domain by aggressing, intimidating, deceiving, or the like. In none of these cases does any such rights-violating activity occur.

Now there is a parallel to the movie-house sneak: someone who attaches a feed to a cable company's line. This we do not defend, for the connection illegally occupies part of the cable. This is *taking* rather than being *given* and demonstrates the possibility of being a bona fide thief in reception as well as in transmission.

Second and quite similar is the notion that our case rests on the ease with which this sort of freeloading may be perpetrated. Again this is not so. We do not plead the liberal notion that "If you leave the door open, you invite theft," but rather the libertarian notion that not all freeloading is theft. If one were to enter an unguarded home, he would illegally occupy another's real property and indeed would be guilty of trespass. That is precisely why the relative ease of basement transmission on owned frequencies is no defense. As we have shown, however, the case with reception is different: Here, the "home" has not been entered at all and no trespass has occurred.

But the notion persists that airwaves are somehow different from other real properties. Let us return to the case of the fireworks display. Is there any philosophical difference between a visible air display dumped on you and an invisible electromagnetic-wave display which carries the programs you capture on your screen? The necessary use of complex receiving equipment in the latter case is surely philosophically irrelevant. If your house were some distance away from the drive-in and you watched with a telescope, would you then be a thief or a "movie pirate"? "Do burglars' tools make the burglary?" we might well respond!

By broadening the rights of pay television companies—after many years of deliberately strangling them—the FCC weakens the individual's right to use his property in entirely permissible ways. This is always the case when new "rights" are granted by the state. Why should we expect airwaves to be any different?

Having said this, we should note that service providers with built-in positive externalities such as these are not, by any means, defenseless. The drive-in can erect a wall, the next-door neighbor can make his display contingent on his neighbor's contribution, and the pay television companies can and are building increasingly sophisticated and impenetrable electronic "fences."

Should broadcasters shield their transmissions? Morally, the question has no answer: They have the right to do so or not to do so as they choose. Financially, they should do so if and only if the added cost of the protective equipment used in both transmission and reception will lose them fewer subscribers than they will gain by welcoming some erstwhile freeloaders into their custom. This becomes a moral consideration only if there is a fiduciary trust, as in a publicly owned corporation. If the market dictates, however, that the shielding is not worth the cost, no one should expect the state to shoulder it. The state already undertakes a multitude of unproductive activities. Why one more?

---

1. See I-2, above.

2. Robert Nozick, "The Principle of Fairness," *Anarchy, State and Utopia* (Basic Books, 1974), pp. 90–95.

6

Scarce Resources

One of the most recurring canards leveled against the market is that it promotes the ravaging of our natural resources by profit-hungry businessmen, fails to urge conservation in the face of scarcity, creates pollution, and otherwise disfigures the natural environment.

Nothing could be further from the truth. As a resource becomes scarcer and scarcer, its price rises in lockstep, thus assuring that wary consumers will conserve. Furthermore, the higher the price, the greater the incentive a businessman has to try to produce more. Finally, alternatives to the resource, once too expensive, are now cheap by comparison. And, as Julian Simon demonstrates in *The Ultimate Resource,* the human mind can always find an alternative which satisfies the same basic need as does a given resource.[1]

When the resource is used in industry, moreover, not only is conservation promoted, but only those producers who can use the resource most efficiently will obtain it. Even after paying the price that scarcity has determined, they must still be able to turn a profit—no mean feat.

As for pollution and disfiguration of the natural environment, these are costs of the production process. But provided third-party effects are adequately remedied, they will be tolerated only so long as the *consumer* believes that the cost of pollution is worth bearing in return for the products he is to receive. The moment people generally believe that what is being produced is not worth the costs to the environment, they will cease paying the premium that those goods must of necessity include in their price to compensate the third parties whose properties are damaged by the production process.

Best of all, the pricing system works automatically, responding to even slight diminutions in the supply and to even slight changes in consumer preferences. The alternative to the market method of dealing with scarce natural resources is a system of allocation and rationing together with protective regulations which can never hope to match the discrimination and immediacy of the pricing system.

---

1. Julian Simon, *The Ultimate Resource* (Princeton University Press, 1981), throughout.

7

Standard Textbooks

Most academic subjects have "standard" textbooks. Here we look briefly and from a free-market perspective at whether standardization is necessarily to be feared as a monopoly in the realm of ideas, a part of the push towards the Politically Correct, and an attack on the traditional professional autonomy that has allowed individual professors to choose their own course materials, or whether it is no such thing.

With the selection of readings as in other domains, it is necessary to distinguish between a coercively established monopoly and a monopoly established through market processes. The standard textbook selected by the marketplace is nothing more fearsome than a consensus, a reflection of a meeting of minds among academics in a particular area about what students should learn and know. After an initial period marked by intense experimentation and competition, the market selects "winners," which then become standards for a generation (generations vary from discipline to discipline). Dissenters still remain free to select from among the other textbooks that flood the market, any one of which may become the standard of the next generation. Indeed, as John Stuart Mill observed, no progress would be possible without continued experimentation at the margins of society[1]—and this is as true of the academy as of society generally. Mill was very far from being a conservative, but his writings are among the most vehemently anti-PC one can find.

In contrast to a market monopoly—a meeting of minds established consensually—stands the collectivist uniformity present when a departmental majority, a committee, or the department head simply assigns textbooks to courses without the consent (and often without the advice) of the instructors in question. It is to be expected that imposed standardization will suffer from the same failures that always beset variants of central planning. Chief among these is that if a mistake is made, it is imposed on everyone. It is surely far superior to let everyone go his own way, mistaken or not, so that the move towards a genuine, consensual standard can proceed unimpeded, guided only by the collective judgment that *spontaneously* arises from *individual* decisions.

The choice is thus not really between standardization and fragmentation. In most fields, several authors stand well above the rest, especially in textbook writing. Rather it is between a spontaneously derived consensual standard that has survived the rigors of the marketplace or an artificially contrived standard that has survived only the scrutiny of some official academic censor, perhaps, even, the majority of one's own departmental colleagues.

---

1. John Stuart Mill, *On Liberty* (Alburey Castell, editor; Appleton-Century-Crofts, 1947), p. 56.

8

Research Funding in the Universities

A major complaint against the federal government in education and research, as in most other areas, is that by taxing, subsidizing, and regulating to achieve social goals it is misallocating resources and undermining the merit system. Thus the focus of conservative ire has been on student aid programs (which are based on need, a socialistic rather than meritocratic principle), on affirmative action programs, on unisex sports requirements, and the like. I wish to suggest that as ill-conceived as these programs may be—and of course ill-conceived they are—they only serve to divert attention from the more insidious and far more harmful effects of government intervention when merit *is* considered.

In these cases, merit is whatever the state says it is. Lately, for example, the traditional requirement of publications for tenure and promotion in the universities has often been supplanted by the requirements of proposal writing and grantsmanship. Even *unfunded* proposals which have not passed the traditional peer review required by most academic journals are regarded as meritorious.

Now this substitution of funding for publication has two implications, one strictly educational, one also political. The educational point, of course, is that it replaces the criterion of an idea's soundness as measured by one's colleagues with the criterion of an idea's marketability, thus biasing research towards development and applications and away from basic ideas and theory. The political point, and I think the more important point, is that since, after all, almost all grants—particularly the grants which provide the colleges with equipment and other overhead—come from the government, it is the government and not the universities which is slowly but surely determining the composition of university faculties. The academy sorely needs fairly objective measures of performance and it is true that tenure and promotion decisions are all too often based on personal factors unrelated to the professor's teaching and research. Still, *that* system at least, as is always true with the free market, allows competition to work its magic: A person to whom one group says "no" may have another group enthusiastically embrace him. When the state is the judge, however, all the deficiencies of centralized decision-making come into play, and the individual not ready, willing, and able to satisfy the government's R & D needs of the moment—or the patience to supply the paperwork required—has no recourse.

We have seen what happens when the state decides who the best educators are and what the best subjects of study are—in the elementary and secondary schools. It would be tragic to allow the same process of bureaucratization and merit determination to infect the better private universities, where at least some learning and scholarship still go on.

To avoid this unfortunate outcome, however, conservatives will have to rethink some basic issues. Is it really always better to contract out research and development to private enterprise (instead of having, say, government defense laboratories), when the risk is the absorption—in effect—of that enterprise? Is it really always better to use merit—rather than need, or simply existence—as the criterion for funding, when that entails state determination of what makes for merit in a student or faculty member? Probably not.

As discussed earlier,[1] it is rare that government subsidizes that which it cannot also control. Unfortunately, this generality has recently come to pass in the grants process as well. It was probably inevitable. We have, for example, recently had Congress "earmark" funds for a large number of universities without using the traditional peer-review process. Academics—of all political persuasions—complained, but to no avail. Government considers itself expert in all matters and, therefore, in no need of a system of refereeing. Another recent development due paradoxically to the budget crunch is the substitution of federal civil servants—who are not qualified to pass on proposals—for expensive outside reviewers in the grants-review process. Merit and deficit-control are two solid conservative issues. But we must guard against their use as a subterfuge for government control of university research programs.

---

1. See I-6, above.

9

Student Activity Fees

During my undergraduate years at The City College of New York in the late 1970s, I had some interesting experiences with student clubs, and I began to re-examine the whole matter of student activities and how they are funded.

There seem to be four ills affecting student organizations which appear to be pervasive on the nation's campuses. First, the members of some clubs share few interests to draw them together. They do understand, however, that any group of students may organize and register with the student government and the college administration and thus receive a portion of the mandatory student activity fees collected by the college at the start of each semester. Thus I recall sitting through a two-hour meeting of a campus honor society where the sole topic of discussion was how to dispose of the generous sum we had been allocated. The debate might still be raging had it not been decided to spend it all on a grand party at the home of a student leader.

The second problem with many student organizations is that the leadership has little incentive to adhere to organizational charters. I recall one prayer-and-snack organization with a charter mandating annual elections. Yet several successive presidents simply appointed the other officers and their successors. When I pointed out to an officer that this was improper, I was asked whether I would prefer the secretariat or the treasury! "Private life," I replied. Of course, nobody really cares enough to take recourse. I didn't. After all, the monies are just there.

Third, club officers frequently divert funds for their own use: pencils, postage, bus fare, meals, maybe a month's rent!

Our student newspaper, *The Campus,* was often filled with the latest scandal—and that's still the case today.

The fourth problem is that mandatory student fees distribute the costs of campus activities with an artificial uniformity. Those who care little about student activities subsidize the average user, while those who are very active are subsidized by the average user. The distribution of benefits is even more artificial. Typically, the student government decides on the apportionment of funds in its own inimitable way. As I recall quite well, this leaves much to be desired.

Now there is quite a simple solution to all these problems. Why not limit student fees to covering such widely used items as the student center, athletics, and the student media? Maybe a piddling sum could be granted to the student government, too, for its advisory role. The remaining student organizations would be funded solely by membership dollars. With the money from student activity fees returned to student pockets, it would be up to the individual whether or not to form, participate in, or pay dues to any club.

Notice how this simple measure addresses all the problems we have sketched. First, clubs whose members share no common bond would quickly dissolve, since their reason for existence—access to mandatory student fees—would be removed.

Second, when the members must pay dues, officers will be held accountable. "Taxation without representation," unless the officers maintain a consensus, would not be tolerated. If members are sufficiently dissatisfied with their club leaders, or with the way their money is being spent, they may simply withdraw along with their financial backing.

Third, the cost of campus activities to each student would depend on how much he used them. But because the overhead of the student activities bureaucracy can be eliminated—including student government oversight functions and some college administration supervision—the typical student user would end up paying less in dues than he saved in fees.

Last, the distribution of student funds would be done naturally, not artificially. The most popular clubs would receive the most money. And no clubs would be indebted to the student government or the college administration for their funds. They would answer only to their members. And that is exactly how it should be.

10

Paradoxical Taxi Fares

Often, I commute to work on Long Island in the wee hours of the morning via so-called gypsy cabs—the unlicensed taxis which abound in my section of upper Manhattan. A flat rate (usually $25 plus tolls) is agreed upon at the start of the trip and is paid at its close. Most of the time, the story ends there.

Sometimes, however, when we pass the airport on the way, an argument ensues. The driver points out that the fare to the airport is more ($35 minimum), yet the cost of that trip measured in time and mileage is less. So, he concludes, he has been had, despite his agreement to the terms and a clear, initial bid on my part stating the time involved (45 minutes) and the destination (Hempstead in Nassau County).

Is he right or wrong? And why? The prime principle of economics is that prices are determined by supply and demand, not costs. Some products may cost a quarter and sell for a half-dollar, while others go for a dollar yet cost only a dime to make. The second producer is neither a profiteer nor an exploiter, and the first producer is neither a benefactor nor a patron. Both producers merely respond to market signals based on supply and demand.

To return to the taxi fare, the market price for a commute to the heart of Nassau County is indeed less than the market price for the shorter, faster trip—in the same direction—to the airport. That this is so evidenced by the very facts of the case: I can always obtain a taxi at the lower rate for the longer, slower trip.

Written in 1988, while a member of the faculty of Hofstra University.

Why this is so is a bit more subtle. A taxi is the only sensible means of travel to the airport, especially during the wee hours of the morning. Commuting, on the other hand, can easily be accomplished by rail—much slower, yet far cheaper—or by car pools with other early risers. Moreover, people are willing to pay more for an occasional trip, when loaded down with baggage, than when they must make the trip several times a week. Finally, the number of gypsies speeding about empty during these hours is very high. Many drivers consider themselves lucky to get *any* substantial fare at that hour. More than a few have gone so far as to suggest a regular contract!

Put in economic terms, the demand for cabs at the time I commute is very low, especially for commuter trips. The choice facing a would-be supplier is often not an airport trip or a commuter's trip, but a commuter's trip or no trip at all (or perhaps a few local trips). Later in the day, during rush hour, when the demand for taxis is far greater, the gap between airport fare and a commuter's fare narrows, for the demand for taxis is far closer to the supply of taxis available for hire.

The law of supply and demand can sometimes appear to have paradoxical results, but if one truly understands the principle and also knows the market situation involved, the paradoxes disappear.

11

The Profit Motive Helps the Homeless

It was Adam Smith who first observed that we are supplied with the wares of the baker and butcher not because of their benevolence, but because of their attending to their own interest.[1]

Frequently, however, charity and relief efforts in a free society do require benevolence. Here, in contrast, I discuss an instance of the invisible hand helping the poor via the profit motive.

Manhattan prides itself on having a 24-hour economy, but there is only one movie theatre, the West Side Cinema duplex, which shows regular fare all night. The West Side Cinema is part of the respected City Cinemas chain of theatres, and charges the same $7 fee that ordinary folk pay throughout the city. Its films have ranged from *Lethal Weapon II* to *The Little Mermaid*.

Depending on how many weeks a feature has been playing, the homeless, often in tattered clothing, occupy from ten to ninety percent of the very-late-night audience. For $7, they are able to obtain shelter and can sleep peacefully, without worry, and in upholstered chairs located within a building that has just been nicely renovated.

The management does not allow this because of benevolence, but because of the profit it makes from selling a night's shelter. Immediately some would be critical and argue that they be given shelter free. But that is simply not possible. The late-night movie-goers who want standard fare can simply not

---

Since the date of this writing, the West Side Cinema has closed; the ownership has declined comment as to why.

support a duplex: They are too few in number, and West Side Cinema would have to close.

As it is, however, the homeless get a better deal than the city gives them, night owls get two choices of movies to see, and the owners are able to pay all their employees (about five) and still turn a profit. I do not go to a very late showing with charitable intentions, but that is the result. The homeless do not sleep peacefully in their places out of concern for my entertainment, but that is the result. Finally, the ownership does not keep the theatre open all night for the benefit of either the homeless or night owls, but again that is the result. The invisible hand brings together three groups, each of which intends only its own benefit, but all of which operate to each other's benefit.

---

1. Adam Smith, *The Wealth of Nations* (Edwin Cannan, editor; University of Chicago Press, 1976), I: 18.

12

The Moral Case for a Balanced Budget

There is much talk these days about balanced budgets, but the talk is about figures when it should be about values, about the economic consequences of imbalance when it should be about its moral propriety. The compelling moral case for a balanced budget—against *both* deficits and surpluses—deserves wider attention.

The earliest American champion of fiscal integrity, Thomas Jefferson, reasoned that "every generation coming equally, by the laws of the Creator of the World, to the free possession of the earth He made for their subsistence, unencumbered by their predecessors, who, like them, were but tenants for life,"[1] "the principle of spending money to be paid by posterity, under the name of funding, is but swindling futurity on a large scale."[2]

With such a principled and honorable heritage, the trillions of dollars of debt we will leave posterity is a betrayal of our origins. We Americans once boldly declared our Republic founded to "secure the blessings of liberty to ourselves and our posterity,"[3] yet today leave each other and our children for generations to come to work off our debts and labor for our continuing prodigality. We Americans who once chafed at the thought that in a land far away others taxed us without our consent, today readily tax those of a time still to come who are not here to withhold their consent and are unable to say nay. What could be plainer than that every bond issue, every deficit, and every "multiplication of the public debt," as it used to be called, amounts to taxation without representation, the very principle against which this nation revolted?

It is not prudence or temperance alone, always good qualities in government, that impels us to forswear deficit financing. It is a matter of right.

The case against surpluses dates to antiquity as witness the Biblical injunction against the accretion of royal wealth.[4] This not only helped preserve the king's character, it served to check depredations of his subjects' holdings. More important, though, and along with the similar injunction against an excessive cavalry,[5] it served to limit his military adventures. The original war chest, accumulated over a long reign by an annual excess of revenues over expenditures, made possible foreign adventures which would have been quite unthinkable if financing them were to have required sudden, confiscatory taxation. As Jefferson remarked, "The present system of war renders it necessary to make exertion far beyond the annual resources of the State, and to consume in one year the efforts of many."

Today, the adventures of state are as often social and domestic as military and foreign, but the principle remains. Governments exist, as John Locke declared, to preserve our property, not to take it from us and store it for some future, unknown mischief. That being so, government is limited to raising revenues for its constitutional purposes.

The argument against surpluses does not apply to the discharge of the public debt, nor does that against deficits apply to the diminution of public reserves. The moral imperative with which we are therefore faced today is for surpluses to gradually eliminate the national debt. But such surpluses must be generated in a manner consistent with our tradition of liberty—i.e., by sweeping tax and regulatory reductions, real fiscal restraint including the wholesale elimination of wasteful government programs, privatization of government enterprises, and the sale of unneeded government properties, not by increased government exactions and confiscatory taxation. That is the course that Jefferson pursued while in public office, and it is the road we must try to regain.

1. Thomas Jefferson, *The Jeffersonian Cyclopedia* (Funk and Wagnalls Company, 1900), p. 369.

2. *Ibid.*

3. Preamble, *Constitution of the United States.*

4. *Deuteronomy 17: 17.*

5. *Deuteronomy 17: 16.*

III. NARROW ETHICS

1

Virtue and Happiness

The life worth living is simultaneously devoted to "the pursuit of virtue" and "the pursuit of happiness." Indeed, it is the principal difficulty of the human condition to resolve the tension between these two overarching life-goals. This is a task we must undertake in what we do in our daily lives. It is also our task here, intellectually.

Two approaches to resolving this tension are possible, the classical and the modern. The classical approach is to find happiness in virtue. The modern approach is to find virtue in happiness. As the reader will find, we are hardly amoral, and although this writing is a part of the modern tradition, the discussion will not degenerate to sloppy nihilism. Indeed, we take it to be no evil to find virtue in happiness, since the laws of nature impel us to seek happiness, and what we are bound to do by our natural condition cannot be immoral. Furthermore, drawing the conceptual categories of crime and impropriety as narrowly as the human mind will allow prevents the state or society from punishing the innocent acting in innocence.

While this unit is partly motivated by its author's strong, libertarian beliefs in limited government, the limitations properly placed on state action in response to what is perceived to be an ethical lapse is only part of the story. There is also the frustrated desire to rectify wrongs done to innocents acting in innocence in the name of ethics. These wrongs generally lack the coercive force of the state, but as John Stuart Mill so clearly shows in *On Liberty*,[1] social sanctions can be just as noxious as state sanctions. Thus we will partly be concerned with the proper limits on social reprobation, limits entirely outside the scope of the libertarian-statist debate.

---

1. John Stuart Mill, *On Liberty* (Alburey Castell, editor; Appleton-Century-Crofts, 1947), throughout.

2

Scandals

It is impossible to read a newspaper or listen to a newscast nowadays and fail to be impressed by the degree to which our society is beset by scandals, large and small. This was not always so. There was a time when scandals were infrequent, if not rare, deviations from the norm. In short, they were scandalous. Today, they are the norm—commonplace and expected.

An exploration of the various causes of this recent and unsettling phenomenon, which we shall undertake here, is necessary if one rejects the conventional wisdom that today's scandals have arisen from the character defects of our current leaders, politicians, and businessmen—who, it is averred, are morally inferior to and more venal than those of yesteryear. In studying news reports over the last few years, several sociopolitical trends largely responsible for the huge increase in indictments precipitated by scandals clearly emerge.

First, there are more requirements and prohibitions set by the law, the courts that interpret them, and the administrative agencies that apply them than ever before. And even where the requirements or prohibitions are longstanding, the focus, energy, and skill brought to their enforcement is a recent development. Naturally, the more laws and regulations there are to be broken, the more violations will occur. And the more effort applied to discovering such violations, the more will be discovered.

It is not that this generation has discovered more *mala in se,* the political theorist's term for acts wrong by their very nature and apprehensible as such to any civilized man. Rather, it is the extreme proliferation of the *mala prohibita,* the designation classically given to acts simply declared crimes by the state. Into this category fall many of the ancient victimless crimes, but also, and even here in capitalist America, many economic "crimes."

For example, it is a *felony* to purchase five percent of a company's stock without notifying the government. This is not only an abridgment of the freedoms of speech and enterprise, it is hardly apprehensible as wrong by its very nature. Even worse, it is also a felony to aid someone's nondisclosure of five percent ownership, by holding the stock for him. What we have here, then, is a situation where a mere bailment is treated as a serious crime, its triviality masked by such terms as "parking securities" and "stock fraud," which to the general public sound so ominous.

Then there are the many burdensome prohibitions and restrictions on mere possession of various substances or other items. And then there are also the many limitations on the peaceful exchange of goods and services between consenting adults. For example, it is felonious for a stockbroker to lend a client more than a specified percentage of the means needed for a securities purchase. What once would have been seen as an act of brotherhood or at least a common business practice has become a "margin violation," punishable by a prison term. Furthermore, when services are exchanged, even between friends, both parties are required to report the service received as barter income or face federal charges. One can't even exchange small favors without the intrusion of the taxman.

On and on the list goes—and we haven't even begun to enumerate the restraints and mandates placed on business enterprises. But the idea is already clear: The index of proscribed and prescribed actions far outstrips the security needed by civilized men to carry out their affairs within the norms of social intercourse. And the longer this irrational and capricious list grows, the longer will be the list of offenders.

Second, there has been an almost unimaginable expansion

of government-sponsored programs, government-funded programs (grants and subsidies), and government regulation of privately sponsored and funded activities. As discussed earlier,[1] such programs provide almost limitless opportunities for abuse, both for the legislators, bureaucrats, and regulators dispensing the funds, permits, or contracts and for the corporations and individuals seeking to receive them. And, both sides, givers and takers, have used these opportunities.

An excellent and timely description of this process comes from William Stern, formerly CEO of New York State's Urban Development Corporation—a huge government agency "that does everything from building convention centers to financing economically depressed mushroom farms." Stern candidly admits that "[t]he fact that government is involved in so much in New York . . . creates the motivation to influence government. And the process of influencing government is always sleazy . . . . It's a side of liberalism that was not predicted, and I think not completely understood . . . . [T]he government becomes very much organized to push through the interests of whoever makes their influence felt."[2]

In other words, the use of what Albert Jay Nock called "the political means" of acquiring wealth—taking it—rather than "the economic means"—earning it—is seductive.[3] By its expansion into all areas of everyday living, government is creating temptations on a massive scale. It is easy enough to fault individuals who succumb to temptation, but one should do so with the full realization that government-wrought temptations are today ubiquitous and overpowering. Thus, it is not that people on both sides of the government dispensary are morally weaker than those of earlier times: The problem is the incredible size and scope of the government dispensary, and the very notion that government may take from A to give to B or regulate the peaceful activities of A in order to benefit B. In pursuit of privileges, official favors, and contracts, people often ignore the rule of law and thereby risk ending both their own careers and the careers of those in government who assist them in return for some form of payoff. Thus, as the daily news reports show us, the existence of the government dispensary with its enormous temptations and corrupting influence is not only theoretically indefensible, it is a very real human tragedy which brings people down at the peak of their powers who otherwise would have lived decent lives and had productive careers.

Third, with the advent of special prosecutors, full-disclosure requirements, and many other similar developments, the intense scrutiny placed on public officials and public figures is greater than that of any previous age. Facilitated by modern transportation, communication, and information processing systems, such scrutiny is urged on us by its "public interest" advocates because of the pervasive corruption discovered in and following the Watergate era. And the more corruption discovered, the more intense is the push for yet more scrutiny.

On the surface, it appears that this trend is not directly caused by the growth of government. After all, scrutiny from the press, encouraged by the very weakened state in which the courts have left libel law in the United States, can be as unrelenting as that of a U.S. Attorney, a state prosecutor, or a legislative panel.

However, closer examination reveals that what has really occurred is the blurring of the all-important distinction between private and public. With almost everything heretofore considered private now considered public, such scrutiny is to be expected. And the continuing attenuation of the distinction between the private and the public is a direct consequence of the growth of government.

Nor is scrutiny itself goal-free. Most of it is directed to discovering whether the person has violated some insignificant *malum prohibitum* or whether he has been involved in the abuse of the government dispensary. Increasingly, also, much scrutiny is directed at the individual's personal life. Only rarely does the scrutiny placed on persons in public life result from suspicion that a ***malum in se,*** unrelated to the government dispensary, has been committed.

In sum, were government's powers to grant subsidies, privileges, contracts, tax exceptions, licenses, and permits sharply curtailed and were government to refrain from declaring peaceful acts illegal, even today's heightened scrutiny would yield little of substance. The public would soon lose interest in reading about probes, inquiries, hearings, and investigations —and scandals would once again be scandalous.

---

1. See I-6, above.

2. Peter Weber, "City of Scams: The Streets Were Paved with Gold Diggers," *National Review,* June 5, 1987, p. 27. The article discusses the corruption scandals in both New York State and New York City, which magnify yet still typify the situation with government in general.

3. Albert Jay Nock, *Our Enemy, The State* (Hallberg Publishing Corporation, 1983), p. 46.

3

"Reforms"

Because of the preoccupation with "scandals" that we have discussed,[1] numerous "reforms" have been undertaken over the last two decades. Unfortunately, many of these tend to bias the composition of the Congress and the other branches of government in such a way as to be inimical to liberty.

First, with the advent of strict limits on outside income, members of Congress and high government officials appointed to office end up viewing the federal government as their principal source of wealth. This is no doubt a partial explanation for the actions of these officers of the State: Laws are passed and regulations are enacted which have the effect of influencing a large number of their constituents to regard the State as their principal benefactor.

Second, full disclosure requirements ensure that only persons with a remarkable degree of personal tolerance of government intervention and invasion of privacy will seek or accept high office. It is all too easy for a man to suppose that what interventions and burdens he can tolerate, his neighbors can and ought to bear as well.

Third, campaign spending limitations and publicly financed campaigns serve to limit the role of private wealth in elections. This means that fewer persons who have acquired wealth in freedom, and are thus favorably disposed to economic freedom, will gain high office. Invariably, those who do not favor economic freedom do favor the political redistribution of wealth and its consequent diminution of freedom.

---

1. See III-2, above.

4

Appearances

Lately the moral focus of our society has been diverted from morality to the avoidance of the appearance of impropriety. The aspiration for untainted appearances is very old; what is new is the scope and force with which it is now applied to everyday living. Thus the Bible states "And ye shall be pure in the eyes of God and man,"[1] and the Talmud explains the verse as an exhortation to the avoidance of both impropriety (purity in the eyes of God) and its appearance (purity in the eyes of man).[2]

Yet a Biblical aspiration to total purity cannot be and ought not to be the standard of morality by which secular society judges its members. Cannot: because man will not live by such a rarefied standard, no matter how forcefully it is proclaimed and applied. Indeed, application of such a standard will simply reveal a thoroughly tainted society, not prevent its appearance. Ought not: because given that man is beset by impurity, such a standard frequently achieves the opposite of that which is intended and various attendant evils.

For example, a faculty member enamored of one of his better graduate students asks her out, but the young lady is already attached and says "No." She then earns a solid B+ on her research paper. Fearing charges of sexual harassment stemming from a clear appearance of impropriety, the professor assigns an A without hesitation. The very wrong to be avoided—an academic action taken on other-than-academic grounds—has occurred, and, in addition, reluctance to further supervise the student's research is likely.

Likewise, a town commissioner responsible for the competitive award of contracts reviews all bids and finds his son-in-law's the most reasonable and worthy. Fearing charges of nepotism and bid-rigging stemming from a clear appearance of impropriety, the public official quickly awards the contract to someone less able. The very wrong to be avoided—non-competitive award of a contract—has occurred, and, in addition, normally irenic family relations have been disturbed.

Finally, an engineering firm with few minority employees and substantial government contracts has a vacancy. The project manager responsible for the hiring decision has two applications, one from an old classmate with whom he already enjoys substantial rapport but who is white, and one from an otherwise equally qualified black. Fearing charges of invidious discrimination stemming from a clear appearance of impropriety, the project manager hires the black applicant. The very wrong to be avoided—a personnel action taken on racial grounds—has occurred, and, in addition, a friendship has been damaged.

All of these cases have in common a plying of principle to avoid the appearance of impropriety, notwithstanding that a real moral wrong is thereby committed. Each also has in common ideas stemming from various movements that arose in the sixties or in the aftermath of the Watergate scandals. In the first case, there are ideas stemming from the intersection of the women's movement and the students' rights movement. In the second case, there are the conflict-of-interest and full-disclosure ideas. And, in the final case, there is the idea of affirmative action and the idea that employment is an entitlement. Thus in each case an ancient aspiration is given life by a modern focus of attention.

Unfortunately, however, our heightened concern with appearances detracts from genuinely moral concerns, shifts the burden of proof to the accused, and erodes basic yearnings for privacy, naturalness, and freedom, all quintessentially American ideals. After all, there is hardly anything more natural than a father-in-law helping a deserving, capable son-in-law, than someone in middle management hiring an old school chum, or than a young professor asking out an attractive graduate student. But, increasingly, people are not socially free to act naturally, even when no wrong is thereby committed and no rights are thereby violated. Accompanying this erosion of freedom and naturalness is a loss of privacy and the presumption of innocence. The mere appearance of impropriety shifts the burden of explanation to people who are neither accustomed nor prepared to defend themselves for natural and reasonable behavior.

Worse still, the explanations offered by such people, no matter how true, how cogent, and how convincing, will be endlessly scrutinized for minor and irrelevant misstatements of fact or lapses of memory and endlessly sifted for improperly resolved conflicts of interest, even when it should be apparent to all that the individual involved acquitted himself honorably.

Conflicts of interest are impossible to avoid. They pervade every area of life, every day of living. But absent evidence to the contrary, it should be presumed that people resolve these conflicts appropriately, since the contrary of this proposition is simply intolerable.

A society as worldly as ours must develop the courage and sophistication not only to condemn that which is wrong, for any self-righteous fool can do that, but also to be silent at that which, contrary to appearances, violates no real moral standard. Such silence requires inner courage, because the temptation to believe, spread, and urge the acceptance of half-true rumors is so overwhelming. It requires sophistication, because to a species that learns almost everything from sight and sound, appearances are so very hard to reject and rumors so very hard to discount. Both require moral discipline and moral discrimination, traits not easily acquired, but whose acquisition is essential for those truly concerned with virtue.

---

1. *Numbers 32: 22.*
2. *Pesachim 13a* and commentaries thereon.

Index

About The Foundation for Economic Education

The Foundation for Economic Education (FEE) is a "home" for the friends of freedom everywhere. Its spirit is uplifting, reassuring, contagious: FEE has inspired the creation of numerous similar organizations at home and abroad.

FEE is the oldest conservative research organization dedicated to the presentation of individual freedom and the private-property order. It was established in 1946 by Leonard E. Read, and guided by its adviser, the eminent Austrian economist, Ludwig von Mises. Both served FEE until their deaths in 1983 and 1973, respectively.

Throughout the years the mission of FEE has remained unchanged: to study the moral and intellectual foundation of a free society and share its knowledge with individuals everywhere. It avoids getting embroiled in heated political controversies raging in Washington, D.C. Located in Irvington-on-Hudson, New York, FEE has remained a purely educational organization.

Since 1956, FEE has published *The Freeman,* an award-winning monthly journal with a long and noble lineage. Under the profound editorship of Paul Poirot it rose to great heights, always fighting for the timeless principles of the free society.

The *Freeman Classics* series of books reflects these heights, consisting of topical collections of great essays and articles published throughout the years. The first three volumes in the series are: *The Morality of Capitalism, Private Property and Political Control,* and *Prices and Price Controls.*

—Hans F. Sennholz